RIMBAUD'S POETIC PRACTICE

RIMBAUD'S POETIC PRACTICE

IMAGE AND THEME IN THE MAJOR POEMS

W. M. FROHOCK

CAMBRIDGE, MASSACHUSETTS
HARVARD UNIVERSITY PRESS
LONDON — OXFORD UNIVERSITY PRESS
1963

Publication of this book has been aided by a grant from the Ford Foundation

Printed in the United States of America

FOR

NORMAN LEWIS TORREY

CONTENTS

RIMBAUD'S POETIC PRACTICE

Introduction

INTERPRETING Rimbaud is a peculiarly hazardous enterprise. We are no longer hampered by defective texts of his work, but the peripheral documents are consistently inconclusive, being mostly letters preserved by chance alone and reminiscences of people who late in life discovered that the poet they had once known was truly great. His family's efforts to keep his name respectable could only lead to more and more obfuscation. Early admirers were more devoted to their private responses to his work than to verifiable fact. All in all, it should surprise no one that the explications of some very attentive critics have often pelted down closed avenues and up blind alleys; the wonder is that we have not gone oftener and much further astray.

In the circumstance it is proper to insist that even the most venturesomely speculative readings of Rimbaud have not been entirely vain. Few of them have failed to add interest to the growing dialogue, and those whose value now seems only heuristic have frequently been the ones to suggest new areas of investigation or possibilities of thitherto unsuspected meaning. But, on the other hand, it is obligatory to add that the proffered "keys" have so regularly stuck in the lock that we have become not only wary of blanket, omnibus interpretations but also exceedingly aware of the perils which await any exegesis, however carefully conducted.

Our wariness and sense of danger have been heightened by the studies of René Etiemble and the late Henri Bouillane de Lacoste.* Quite apart from what they may, or may not, have shown us about Rimbaud, they have enlightened us immensely about ourselves and the conditions in which we work. Etiemble's demonstration that critics have already found several thousand ways of saying something wrong—and often silly—about Rimbaud cannot but inhibit even the most courageous: the possibility of adding to the total is unpleasantly real. And although Bouillane de Lacoste's effort to redate the works by the development of the poet's handwriting has left numerous expert readers unconvinced, it has made us realize just how fragile our knowledge of Rimbaud is. If there is not enough evidence to put beyond challenge his point that the *Illuminations* were written later than *Une Saison en enfer,* the same absence of evidence prevents conclusive refutation.

Thanks to these two scholars we have become permanently suspicious of any neatness and symmetry appearing in the parabolas we draw to represent Rimbaud's poetic career. Not long ago the same symmetry seemed unassailable and complete. So was our confidence in affirming it. The young poet had

* For comment on these and other works upon which this discussion has drawn, see the Bibliographical Note, page 239.

begun, we said, by imitating the poets of his time. Then, while kept virtually a prisoner by a war and a repressive mother, he had discovered a technique for dislocating the elements of the ordinary world of experience and reassociating them in an imagery which revealed previously unsuspected relationships between phenomena—if not, as he claimed, the Unknown itself. This technique, according to us, had been announced in the "Lettre du voyant," tried out the following year, and been pushed to its ultimate possibilities in the *Illuminations*, in which Rimbaud even confused himself with God. After this, we were sure, he had fallen back, as he had said he might do, full of the bitter despair and failure which he proceeded to orchestrate in *Une Saison*, his farewell both to poetry and to misspent youth. And thenceforward there was only the enigmatic "man with the wind in his heels," wandering over the world until at last, ill and long absent and forgotten, and having himself forgotten even the titles of his own poems, he came home to die. This was what we believed yesterday.

Today we are much readier to distinguish between what we imagine and what we know. But we are still unable to leave Rimbaud in peace. Ours is a generation of interpreters: we deal in what we call "levels of meaning"; we find allegory everywhere; the literature we love must be obscure and secretive. Rimbaud's writing is full of hidden significance, and begs for interpretation as much as it defies it. For manifold reasons, some of which may be only indirectly connected with his poetry, he is inordinately important to us.

Everyone seems to have been able to find something for himself—or of himself—in this poet. Paul Claudel's discovery of a source of spiritual sustenance in *Une Saison* is hardly more surprising than that the Surrealists should have claimed Rimbaud as their precursor: *Une Saison* is just as certainly the product of a religious crisis, in part, as it is, again in part, a rejection of literature such as Surrealism advocated. Sensitive readers have been persuaded that its author had an angel in him; others, equally sensitive, have seen him as the eternal juvenile delinquent. In one of his recentest incarnations he appears as the master of modern revolt — one who, having found his world intolerable, pronounced a *non serviam* which has been echoed by writers as different from each other as Bernanos, Céline, Camus, and Ezra Pound. His work, and even more his example, has given abundant aid and comfort to people as politically involved as the Communists, and to those as detached from politics as the recent Beat Generation. He has been taken for another Nietzsche fabricating a morality of freedom, and for another Tolstoi all athirst for universal love.

He could not have failed to impress many as a prototype of that favorite hero figure of recent European intellectuals, the metaphysical Adventurer. This is a man who, because life in Europe has lost its savor, goes off to a remote and savage region to find satisfaction, and perhaps a fitting death, in violent activity. He is said to want to "put a scar on the map." Either he dies, like Conrad's Mister Kurz or Malraux's Perken, the protagonist of *La Voie royale*, or else, like the tycoon Ferral, in Malraux's *Condition humaine*, he survives to realize that his life has no significance beyond that of his adventures. He is both fictional and historical: Roger Stéphane's *Portrait de l'aventurier* names T. E. Lawrence, Ernst von Salomon, and Malraux himself as typical cases; in fiction as in history he has the same characteristic traits — the ability to generate a legend of himself, an aura of dark doings and even perhaps of crime, and inscrutable motives.

Simultaneously we see Rimbaud as having enacted one of the parables of our time. We have told ourselves repeatedly the story of an adolescent who lives through some halcyon moment, infinitely preferable to ordinary life, but then somehow lets his idyl escape him; he tries desperately to recover it; eventually he finds either that he is unable to do so at all, or else that when recovered his idyl is idyllic no longer. Rimbaud's version is in the introduction of *Une Saison en enfer*, where he declares that he has lost the key to a "Great Party" and is trying to find it again. The story puts him at the head of a line of heroes who may be as unlike each other as the central characters in *Le Grand Meaulnes* and *The Great Gatsby* but who share his — and, we are told, our — resistance to growing up. Whether or not it really helps us understand Rimbaud is a question; we may simply be imposing an image of ourselves upon him; but there is no doubt at all that it helps us understand ourselves.

We also cherish an image of him as the explorer-poet who first discovered the limits of poetry and, having asked of it more than poetry could provide, abandoned literature entirely. Once more what we imagine may not be entirely in accordance with the facts. It is not absolutely certain that Rimbaud had stopped writing completely by 1875, and it is even less so that he exhausted the possibilities of his vocation. The chapters following here will present the case that what happened was the reverse — poetry exhausted Rimbaud. But a century which has seen the Surrealists abjure all poetic intentions, and a later generation develop literary styles for which it claimed the merit of being "nonliterary" and even "antiliterary," would naturally clasp him to its heart. One understands why, as Etiemble complains, the Surrealists tried to "annex" him; if Rimbaud was not in fact their ancestor, we must at least admit a trace of family resemblance. And one need not have been a Surrealist to have speculated about the ultimate fate of literature in our culture and to have found Rimbaud's experience relevant.

We have even a fourth major reason to think of him as

especially important: we recognize him as one of the great discoverers of the irrational regions of the human psyche. The "Lettre du voyant" is a brilliant declaration of the creativeness of the areas of the mind not subject to conscious censorship. What numerous others had hinted at, but practiced only on occasion and very tentatively, Rimbaud placed at the exact center of his work. His conception of the poetic personality—the celebrated "JE est un autre"—sounds more and more as one meditates upon it like a first groping statement, made without the help of technical vocabulary, of the separateness of the superego from the id. He was too turned in upon himself and exclusively focused on his own experience, to use this discovery as an instrument for probing into motive, such as a new generation would shortly use to change the nature of much fiction, some poetry, and no little drama. His personal interest in hallucination, and the uses he thought he could make of it, probably imposed a limit on his insight. But in psychology, as in so many other matters, he speaks to us in a language more intelligible to our moment than to his own. We honor him accordingly.

In all such elective sympathies and identifications of ourselves with a figure of the past there is an undeniable element of myth. Doubtless Rimbaud would not seem so close to us if instead of clearing out of Europe he had chosen to stay at home and continue writing poetry. Some of what we know about his years in Abyssinia makes him sound less like a heroic adventurer than like a petty bourgeois who was willing to undergo hardship in order to assure a later retreat into snug security at home. His complaint about the lost key may have been the expression of a passing mood. And Freud himself has testified to the number of European writers in whom could be found intimations of the new psychology. In the matters because of which we find him so important Rimbaud was hardly unique and hardly an initiator. Why should we select him, especially, as a subject for such admiration?

Myths do not accrete upon the biographies of all poets, however great they are held to be. That they did so upon Rimbaud's is evidence that he was born possessing the secret of Delphi, which was the secret of being infinitely suggestive. Suggestiveness, which, according to the late Margaret Gilman's *Idea of Poetry in France,* was the ideal which had gradually replaced controlled eloquence by Baudelaire's time, alone permitted Rimbaud to be so many things to so many men. And since suggestiveness is a quality of poetry, the ultimate sources of his appeal to us must be sought in the peculiar nature of the poetry itself.

Although the commonplace that Rimbaud is one of the two sources from which French poetry developed for most of a century must be qualified to the extent of admitting that much of what came later was already implicit in the work of Baudelaire, it seems accurate to say that after Baudelaire the main stream divided. There was Rimbaud. There was Mallarmé.

We have come to think of Mallarmé as the incarnation of poetic purity. His characteristic poem is a distillate. He discovers new properties in the accepted word and new possibilities of expression in the accepted form. His manipulations of syntax reveal the importance of syntax, its delicacy as an instrument, the hopelessness of revolt against it, its indispensability. He is, as we see him today, the poet of the planned, calculated, superintended poem and the model for all who work out their salvation through discipline. We read him with the expectation of being rewarded by meanings which, far from being our invention — the product of our response to the poem — have been explicit in the poem itself from the beginning, no matter how hidden among its intricacies.

When Mallarmé intends a symbol, one may doubt one's understanding of it but hardly the poet's intention of making one. The swan frozen in the ice raises no suspicion that "Le Vierge, le vivace et le bel aujourd'hui" reflects a concern about the effect of cold on aquatic birds. Our confidence is absolute that the swan stands for something which is not a swan and which, with attention, can be identified. Furthermore, the ice in which the bird is frozen will acquire its meaning from the bird's identity. So, in turn, will the flight that the paralyzing ice inhibits, and after these the other elements of the sonnet will fall into place in a determined symbolic structure. A failure of our discernment in no way implies the absence of something to discern: the difficulty is part of the poem's intended total effect—and one easily accepts the story about Mallarmé's having told Degas that a certain poem was finished "except for adding the obscurity."

In Mallarmé's descendants, of whom Valéry is the most obvious example, the poem sometimes approaches the character of a rebus. One treats a piece like the "Cimetière marin" as though it were a puzzle to be solved. The equation of roof with sea, in the first stanza, is meant to resist immediate perception: why should a roof "palpitate" between pines and tombs? Only gradually, and in a measure that the poet rigidly controls, does the equivalence emerge. And this is the characteristic procedure of the poem: the reader advances as he is led to recognize one metaphor after another. Thus among his pleasures are those of playing an elevated intellectual game, and of witnessing the calculated artistry of a poet who is also, in a sense, his opponent. It is true that Valéry, with his theories of poetry as intellectual exercise, is an extreme case, but he is emblematic of a generation which included prose writers like Gide as well as poets, who learned from Mallarmé a devotion to technique.

It is only natural that Mallarmé should be a hero to a time that identifies the poet primarily as an artist and artistry with technical mastery. Rimbaud's sharing our attention with him suggests at first a complete polarization of the poetic tendencies of such a moment. It is not, after all, true that he and Mallarmé were complete polar opposites. Mallarmé is far from being devoid of suggestiveness; Rimbaud is far from being totally indifferent to poetic form—in fact, if we were not so sure of his essential competence in form we should be much less impressed by his having found it, eventually, inadequate to his needs. But it is no less a fact that we do revere Mallarmé for making poetry an art of quintessences, and Rimbaud for making it a means of metaphysical and psychic adventure.

For Rimbaud is, for us, the poet of multiple meanings, often of contradictions, always of ambiguities—a poet of richness. Where Mallarmé's work seems superintended and controlled, Rimbaud's strikes us, in contrast, as approaching spontaneous and uncensored utterance. With Mallarmé we equate the intellect, but with Rimbaud, the subconscious. And whereas Mallarmé's symbols appear to be elements in a special system of communication, Rimbaud's appear to be equally susceptible to widely varying interpretations.

He speaks in *Une Saison en enfer*, for example, of an "Orient" where, we gather, life may be infinitely preferable to the life he has known in Europe. Rimbaud's Europe being a geographical fact, the reader looks automatically for his Orient to be one also. He has been taken to mean not merely Asia but India, and his poems have been searched for possible debts to Hindu philosophy. But restricting the word's sense in this way adds nothing to the meaning of the poem; instead, it adds one more unwieldy element to an already cumbersome amount of material whose value is, at best, speculative. The reader is forced to return to what little he actually knows, which is something essentially negative: Rimbaud is desperately unhappy in Europe, that is, the Occident, and is persuaded that somewhere outside the world as he is familiar with it there must be some better place, not Europe and not the Occident but their opposite and thus an Orient. The word is not the name of a place but a synonym for his dissatisfaction or a symbol to express his infelicity.

There are many such symbols in his work. The present chapters will be occupied with them frequently, as must any study of Rimbaud, because their ambivalence—often, their polyvalence—is a principal source of the wealth of possible meaning which has permitted such varying readings of his poems and which sets him at the pole opposite Mallarmé. These symbols are, of course, constant incitements to error. An interpretation that accepts one suggestion of a symbol as being uniquely valid, in exclusion of all the others it contains, cannot avoid being warped and one-sided. It would seem elementary that as we venerate Mallarmé for being one kind of poet and approach him with methods of exegesis appropriate to his kind, just so we should approach Rimbaud with methods applicable to the particular kind of poet our admiration shows him to be.

In intention at least this is such a study. With all due deference to its predecessors which have treated Rimbaud as one of the most complex of poets, it proposes an approach which exploits the poet's simplicity. It does not deny that in numerous ways Rimbaud was very complex indeed; but it affirms that there was one way in which he was not complex—and that this is self-evident not from a biography which may be changed at any future moment by some new discovery but from the poems themselves. For however far Rimbaud may take us into the study of Freud, the Cabala, Eastern philosophy, or the behavior of delinquent adolescents, he remains always the poet of "O saisons, ô châteaux," whose principal pursuit was "the magic study of happiness." It is characteristic of our time that critics have battled over the appropriate placing of a comma in this poem with far more energy than they have dispensed in deciding what Rimbaud is talking about here, and more especially what he means by *bonheur*. Until some more convincing reading of the passage comes along, we had better accept the obvious one: that he identifies the practice of poetry with the search for felicity, or for what in some contexts might be called beatitude. Complex in so many ways, in this one Rimbaud is essentially, even embarrassingly, simple. That is, the range of motive in his poetry is extremely narrow.

By motive is meant the elemental and hidden subject of a poem as discriminated from its ostensible one. For example, the ostensible subject of "Ulysses" is the proposal of one last exploit which an old chieftain addresses to his veteran followers. The motive, as opposed to this, is Tennyson's respect and admiration for indomitability in the face of old age. For an example closer home, the ostensible subject of "Le Bateau ivre" is the adventure of the poet-boat through scenes that never were on land or sea; the motive, on the other hand, is a defeated effort to gain and retain a particular form of felicity.

In a number of poems so large that they comprise a major portion of his output, Rimbaud's motives are precisely two: feeling good or not feeling good, felicity or the absence of felicity. In a number more, he is occupied with a transition from one state to the other, and in still others the subject is something upon which happiness depends or by which unhappiness is caused. In a poem like "Sensation," in which the poet imagines walking along a path through wheat on a cool summer evening, felicity alone is the motive; in "Le Cœur supplicié" the motive is unadulterated unhappiness; poems like "Mémoire" and "Larme" record a transition. The poems about war and politics have the same motive but reveal it indirectly (for example, war is bad because it keeps him from being happy). Felicity and infelicity were, by inspection, the ultimate polar terms of his awareness of life during the years when he was writing poetry. Felicity, for him, includes the range from mere physical well-being—he is the only poet who comes to mind as having celebrated in verse the relief of a distended bladder — to something like the ecstasy of the mystic; infelicity runs a gamut from momentary distaste to a cosmic revolt not entirely unlike the revolt of Milton's Satan.

Such is the sense in which Rimbaud can be said to be simple. Quite obviously a study oriented toward these motives will reveal little, if anything, about poems like "Voyelles" and certain of the *Illuminations*; with respect to the poems in which Rimbaud attains a considerable degree of detachment, so that his deeply personal concerns are not involved, such an approach is bound to be fruitless. But it happens that there are few such poems in the Rimbaud canon and that they are not the ones over which interpreters debate most, over which the most critical energy is expended, and in which we are most deeply interested.

It is also self-evident that the behavior of the creative imagination is as subject to the workings of habit as is any other kind of human behavior, although in individual instances the fact may not be entirely easy to demonstrate. I have tried to show elsewhere how the fictions of André Malraux, from his earliest Surrealist fantasies down to the *Noyers de l'Altenburg*, repeatedly organize events into a pattern which Toynbee would call "Withdrawal–Enlightenment–Return." Toynbee has no corresponding term for the pattern that turns up as consistently in Rimbaud's writing as "Withdrawal–Enlightenment–Return" does in Malraux; for convenience let it be called "The Defeated Enterprise." The "Enterprise" refers, of course, to the poet's wild pursuit of happiness, noted above. "Defeated" is justified by the fact that his imagination returns regularly to the frustration of the pursuit.

This proposed procedure seems simpler than it is in fact. Before Rimbaud has advanced very far in his poetic career he begins to identify the search for happiness with the process of making poetry; as early as "Le Bateau ivre" happiness appears to him to be available through poetry when all other accesses are closed off, and the purpose of the poet is to achieve the state of insight and special knowledge which Proust later thought of as "privileged moment" and James Joyce as "epiphany." It is logical at this point that the failure of the seeker of happiness and the failure of the poet in his poem should also become identical.

But why should Rimbaud have been so constantly preoccupied by the possibilities of failure? It is not difficult to show that he was haunted by them from the beginning, that in devising his celebrated poetic program with its systematic disorientation of the senses he virtually guaranteed the collapse of his project, and that, almost certainly, he suspected as much. Felicity had come to reside in the contemplation of an image — and it was characteristic of the state he put himself into in his quest for "voyancy" that the image should not abide to be contemplated.

The authority for such an understanding as this of Rimbaud's work derives from the poems themselves, and may be accepted or rejected by the individual reader according to whether or not he sees in them what I see. I am indebted, as we all are, to the devoted editorial work of Bouillane de Lacoste, Jules Mouquet, and Suzanne Bernard, and am deeply beholden to Enid Starkie's biography. I have followed Miss Starkie slavishly in every matter of established fact. Where she speculates, I have put her speculations in the same category as my own, and have looked with the same suspicion on hers as on mine. The same may be said for the use I have made of Emilie Noulet's *Premier Visage de Rimbaud.*

An observant reader may notice that I have tried to avoid reading back from later utterances of Rimbaud to explain earlier ones. The poet's distressed commentary on his work in the "Alchimie du verbe" chapter of *Une Saison en enfer* is an excellent document on how he felt about his poetry at that writing, but is not dependable testimony on his disposition when he actually wrote the poetry: we do not even know if he remembered at all accurately either how he felt at the moment of creation or what his intentions then were; in view of how undependable his memory was in other ways, we might even do well to assume that he did not. Similarly, it is absolutely impossible to accept with even minimal confidence "Les Poètes de sept ans" as a document on the child Rimbaud's disposition toward his mother; it is a trustworthy one, however, on the feelings he held toward her as he approached seventeen. This is not a matter of being unwilling to "believe" Rimbaud: it is one thing to accept whatever he says about himself in those instances where one can discover what he means and what one is supposed to believe, but quite another to give his utterances an extension which he did not authorize, either in matters such as those just mentioned or in assuming, as so many readers of the "Lettre du voyant" have done, that when he said "Inconnu" he meant God. To such extravagance I have preferred accepting the limitations imposed by the texts themselves, even when the latter are not satisfactorily communicative.

My own interest in Rimbaud is both aesthetic and psychological, although probably more the former than the latter; I have, in any case, stayed as far away from psychology as seemed possible. That many of the poems report what might well be described as waking dreams I have no doubt, and one is forced to deal with dream content if one is to deal with the poems at all, but I have stopped short of studying the dream mechanisms themselves for two reasons which to me seem adequate. First, I doubt that we know about Rimbaud anywhere near what we should to make serious analysis possible. Second, such activities are for qualified professionals only. Cecil A. Hackett's psychoanalytical explications of Rimbaud are extremely interesting, but the interest is speculative.

So far as has been possible I have tried to avoid forcing "total readings" of the poems upon the reader, preferring to confine myself to the question of what the poems are *about* and to leave him free, otherwise, to interpret them for himself. I assume him to be English-speaking, somewhat familiar with French literature, interested in poetry in general and unsatisfied with his ability to penetrate the poems in question here. If, in addition, he is also somewhat bewildered and made impatient, like me, by the remarkable welter of Rimbaud criticism, so much the better. The aim of the present study is to make the pleasure of reading Rimbaud available to him.

Chapter I – Poetry as Wish Fulfillment

THE COMMONEST critical practice assigns everything Rimbaud wrote before his final break with home to a single, more or less preliminary, stage of his development. On the testimony of the poetry itself, however, it is reasonably clear that he passed through four different phases. There was first a timid but eager young poet who composed set pieces. Then came the adolescent vagabond of the fugues.* After this we have the surly young captive, condemned to the confinement of Charleville by his mother through the winter of 1870–1871. And finally there is the fledgling Prometheus who, after falling upon

* Because English appears to lack a single word for the compulsion to run away I am adopting the French one. Accounts of these escapades figure prominently in all the biographies. Correspondence quoted may be found in the Pléiade edition under dates indicated. The chronology of Rimbaud's life in the same edition will also be found helpful.

the notion of the poet's function which he outlines in the "Lettre du voyant," implores his friend Demeny to destroy all the earlier work and proceeds to write new poems like "Le Bateau ivre." The ultimate legitimacy of dividing any talent into so many fractions is, of course, dubious; we know that human development is not rectilinear and that it is continuous. The risk of sacrificing truth to neatness and convenience is worth taking in Rimbaud's case, but only because, from being so fragmented, his talent appears in an unaccustomed and revealing light.

"Anch'io," Rimbaud wrote Théodore de Banville on May 24, 1870, "I, too, shall be a Parnassian." What he really meant was that he wanted to be a poet; Parnassian and poet were synonyms; to be one was to be the other. He was not thinking of the Parnassians as a special school: he wanted to be one just as he wanted also to be a "true Romantic" and a "descendant of Ronsard." As literary criticism the letter is thus somewhat blurry. Rimbaud is not concerned with nice distinctions or, indeed, even with factual accuracy: he adds a few honorific months to his age. What emerges most clearly is his consuming need to appear in print. He wants mightily to be included in the next issue of the *Parnasse contemporain*, and his use of the future tense suggests not only that one is not a Parnassian, for him, until one's poems have found their place in the publication, but also that until one has been published somewhere one is not a poet at all.

This thirst for recognition was not new. When, two years earlier, he had mailed off a congratulatory poem of sixty Latin hexameters for the young Prince Imperial's first communion, the act had been secret but the poem had been signed and had borne a return address; he had been publicly thanked for it. A year later he had contributed his first verses in French — the first to have survived at any rate — to the *Revue pour Tous*:

"Les Etrennes des orphelins" appeared in the number of January 2, 1870. There is even a chance that still another poem, "Les Trois Baisers," printed in *La Charge* in August 1870, had been written and mailed before Rimbaud wrote Banville to announce his existence and ambition.

The urge was also to prove durable. There is no shred of evidence that so long as he went on writing poetry Rimbaud ever wanted to hide his light. The image of a poet who characteristically lost interest in whatever he wrote as soon as he finished it has no more foundation than the word of his brother-in-law, the egregious philistine, Paterne Berrichon, who habitually put middle class respectability above the truth. Doubtless Rimbaud became less single-mindedly intent on publishing as time went on. The disturbances of his productive years—those caused by the war and those to be blamed upon his own instability—would be reason enough for that. He was also too wretchedly poor to be able to publish at his own expense. While it is very true that in his lifetime his poems did not see general circulation, it is just as true that he tried to circulate them, that he was forever working over his manuscripts and copying them out for his teacher Izambard, his friend Demeny, for Banville, for Verlaine; he initialed his contributions to the manuscript *Album Zutique*; he seems to have had some interest, as late as 1875, in publishing the *Illuminations*. (This last testimony comes from Verlaine, whose memory may not always have been dependable, but it has never been discredited, and the assumption that Rimbaud jettisoned his manuscript is based largely upon our ignorance of what his disposition toward it really was.) There is no room to doubt, more particularly, that what he wanted most in 1870 was to see his name and work on paper, to be a poet like other poets.

At sixteen years and some months he sounds uncommonly like millions of other young victims of the literary urge. He is eager not so much to *do* something as to *be* something, and no more to *be* something, perhaps, than to *be known* as something; what he wants is public, a status. The letter to Banville, like the "Lettre du voyant" which he will write not many months later, is a performance. "We are in the month of love," he writes, "and I am seventeen. It's the age of hopes and dreams, as they say—and here I am, a child touched by the Muse's finger—excuse me if this is banal—beginning to speak the things I believe, my hopes, my sensations, all these poetic things—I call that springlike." The indulgent Banville should be excused if, perhaps, he smiled at such a self-conscious bit of showing off: he can hardly have failed to see that Rimbaud is his own first audience here and probably his most attentive one.

2

The three poems he enclosed in the letter are performances also. Two of them—"Ophélie" and "Soleil et chair"—conform resolutely to the Parnassian aesthetic: the subjects are distant from the actual concerns of life; the absence of authentic personal involvement is almost ostentatious; the imagery is plastic. The other, "Sensation," is too short to judge in this respect, and its experiential content is perfectly available to anyone able to stroll across the fields at evening, but surely it violates no canon then current nor introduces anything unfamiliar to habitual readers of the poetry of the time. Like the other two, "Sensation" is a set piece. If one wants to be a poet, then one must behave as poets do: all three poems give evidence of a capacity for poetic behavior. The exercise is essentially the same one that Proust's Marcel engages in over a much longer period: he feels the vocation to write and spends years going through the motions before the day when he steps backward upon the loose cobblestone, the floodgates of involuntary memory are opened, and his mode of existence changes from being something to doing something.

Academic scholarship has found in these, as in all of Rimbaud's early poems, a concert of echoes from contemporary, or slightly earlier, poets. Such discoveries lead to the conclusion that Rimbaud was practicing what the French call "secondary literature" — writing which feeds on other writing. Possibly we would see clearer what was happening, and judge more appositely, if our current doctrines of poetry did not so firmly deprecate such imitation. In a sense Rimbaud's early writing is indeed highly imitative. But what else, in the circumstances, could it have been? The notion he could have of what poets did was necessarily formed from the example of those he happened to know; there was no means of knowing that the given samples were not totally representative. Rimbaud was still a schoolboy, and his practice here is an extension of what goes on in schools — the master sets a subject and the pupil's success is determined by his response to that particular stimulus, staying within the rules which education inexorably sets up. Rimbaud had been particularly clever at composition in Latin verse, had received prizes in it, had seen his work and name appear in the schoolmasters' trade journal. Now he was doing something similar, in French instead of Latin, with the difference that he took subjects set not by individuals but by the practice of the moment.

Eventually what he was saying would become more important to him than the fact of his saying it. Then, and only then, could he change from serving an image of himself to serving an ideal of poetry. The change, in his case, would be slow of completion: even as late as *Une Saison en enfer* his self-contemplation cannot always be distinguished from narcissistic posturing. Until the change begins to take place he stays necessarily in his first phase — the phase of set pieces.

Eight of the ten poems he wrote before the first fugue take subjects directly reminiscent of poets ranging back from Swinburne all the way to Villon: the plight of a family of children whose mother has abandoned them to a cold and hostile world ("Les Etrennes des orphelins"); youthful sexual experience ("Première soirée); the enslaved and downtrodden turning upon their masters ("Le Forgeron"); the neopagan refrain that the world was better when young, joyous, fertile, and unblighted by Christianity ("Soleil et chair"); the calm beauty of a maiden untimely dead ("Ophélie"); how good it is to be outdoors on a pleasant evening ("Sensation"); a *danse macabre* ("Le Bal des pendus"); an Invitation to the Voyage ("Les Réparties de Nina"). And a reasonably good case can be made for putting the other two poems in the same category.

If the Tartufe in "Le Châtiment de Tartufe" represents the superficially pious burghers whom Rimbaud holds to make up a class of philistines and exploiters, then the "Méchant" who strips Tartufe naked may be taken to represent the disinherited in revolt, Tartufe becomes an emblematic figure like the King in "Le Forgeron," and we are once again contemplating a much-treated commonplace. Similarly, if the modern marine Venus, rising from the waves of her zinc tub and repulsive with her folds of fat and her ulcer, is taken to represent the tired and ugly modern world as contrasted with the clean and wholesome beauty of some ancient one, then "Vénus anadyomène" returns to the subject of "Soleil et chair." Even if these earliest poems are not all set pieces in exactly the same sense and to the same degree, the proportion is still impressive: eight out of ten clearly have something of the poetic exercise about them, and the two remaining may, if one wishes, be read as if they had it, also.

This is not to affirm, of course, that the break was absolute. Rimbaud did not completely give over exploiting such subjects after his first fugue. "Le Dormeur du val," for example, exhumes the ancient equation of death with sleep, and the "Effarés," while a more memorable poem than "Les Etrennes des orphelins," is, like the latter, a poem about pitiful children in cold weather. But the proportion of poems devoted to such commonplaces diminishes once Rimbaud has made the decisive step of taking the train toward Paris. He will be less concerned, afterwards, with proving to himself — and to whatever part of the world may be interested — that he is a poet, and correspondingly more concerned with the actual poetry he is writing.

3

If Rimbaud had written no more than these poems of the first phase he would be completely and deservedly forgotten; they owe their place in today's anthologies to what he was to write later. Yet they are essential for understanding the later work, because while in one sense he is "not yet Rimbaud," in another he is already the Rimbaud he will always be.

Even now his chief concern is felicity, the criterium he invokes instinctively to measure human experience. Either one is happy and life is correspondingly good, or else one is unhappy and life is correspondingly bad. Generally — though not always, for there will be poems like "Les Effarés" — the happiness or unhappiness he contemplates will be his own. As he grows older its specific outlines will change. He will equate it with the euphorias of the "Lettre du voyant" and "Le Bateau ivre," with the epiphanies objectified in the landscapes of the *Derniers vers* of 1872 and of the *Illuminations*. The practice of poetry will become indistinguishable from the search for beatitude. His complaint in *Une Saison en enfer* will be that poetry has not made him happy. Furthermore, the elements of which felicity is made will not vary for him either, at least as to their essence, although of course his notion of them will become more complex with passing time. They will never evolve beyond a point where they may be recognized easily as contact with nature, a feeling of freedom, and an expansive state which he will call love.

At the point in his life that interests us now the prescription for felicity is not at all complex. In "Sensation" little more is needed than the "blue summer evenings."

> Par les soirs bleus d'été, j'irai dans les sentiers,
> Picoté par les blés, fouler l'herbe menue:
> Rêveur, j'en sentirai la fraîcheur à mes pieds.
> Je laisserai le vent baigner ma tête nue.
>
> Je ne parlerai pas, je ne penserai rien:
> Mais l'amour infini me montera dans l'âme,
> Et j'irai loin, bien loin, comme un bohémien,
> Par la Nature, – heureux comme avec une femme.

Here nature is a direct and pleasurable stimulation of the senses. It consists of things to be felt: the wheat, the young grass, the cool breeze. Everything is sensation: the grain picks like a chicken; the turf gives succulently underfoot; the earth cools the soles of the feet; the wind bathes the head. The first stanza is one sustained sensual response.

And the response is what counts. Even at this early moment, the young poet is less interested in nature's concrete specificities than in their effect upon himself. The verbs he uses are revealing: he will be the object of the pecking and the recipient of the coolness; he will be the one washed by the wind. His nature exists because he is in it.

We call him one of the great nature poets, and doubtless he is one. But nature poets are variously disposed toward their subject. An Emily Dickinson is attentive to the individual bee, the particular flower, the singular and special red leaf of autumn – to a degree such that once she rejects the use of the common collective noun and wishes she were "a hay." For a Thoreau nature is an immense reservoir of passionately interesting fact, which is material to be learned and known. Wordsworth's nature is chiefly a setting for the soul, perhaps, but in the "Prelude" he is capable of distinguishing between two species of ash tree; he is aware of the particulars of his setting, even though he may see them from a distance. Rimbaud is entirely different from all three.

In all his work he rarely names a flower, and when he does do so it is even rarer that he gets its name right: his gladioli turn out to be wild flag, not gladioli, and his heliotropes must, from the context, be sun flowers. This characterizes his attitude. What he apprehends in nature will be what modifies his sensations directly; when she has no effect upon him he lets her languish. In "Soleil et chair," written no more than two months later than "Sensation," and in which he is intentionally adopting a prescribed posture in his bid to please Banville, we shall see him leave her absolutely lifeless.

Clearly, here is one poet who will not often be capable of the pathetic fallacy. True, in "Ophélie" he makes the water cradle the drowned maiden, the wind kiss her breasts, and willows weep upon her shoulder. But these personifications are manifestly produced for the occasion, and lack the persuasiveness of his poems in which nature is not to be distinguished from climate and its effect upon the awakened senses. Eventually, in the *Illuminations*, he will become so preoccupied with the internal responses that the reader can only guess what has stimulated them; this kind of inwardness will leave ellipses which are a principal source of his obscurity. What we see in "Sensation" is the beginning of a long process.

Love, in these earliest poems, takes the form of simple and rather vague erotic feeling. This fact has greatly complicated the task of Rimbaud's biographers. More has been written about his sexual make-up, perhaps, than about any other single aspect of his life. Few doubt, today, that he was actively homosexual. Yet the image of love presented by the poems written before his strange idyl with Verlaine implies, in so far as it implies anything at all, a completely normal orientation. "Première soirée" and "Les Réparties de Nina" openly celebrate the love of women, and the love is explicitly physical. The Aphrodite of "Soleil et chair" is abundantly female. Rimbaud's friends, in particular Ernest Delahaye, were persuaded that some girl or other had played a role in the poet's early sentimental life and that she had even participated in one of his escapades. The erotic phantasies of "Roman" and "A la musique," poems which belong to his second rather than his first phase but are relevant to the present topic, are patently directed at women. In the poems written before the spring of 1871 only one suggests something else: "Mes petites amoureuses" rejects heterosexual love with an intensity little less than sadistic.

A conjecture has long been on the market that an unfortunate experience—homosexual rape, to be exact—which Rimbaud is supposed to have met with in Paris in May 1871 determined his tottering sexual allegiance. But there is no objective evidence that the event actually took place and, in spite of the inordinate amount that has been written on and around it, our knowledge adds up to little. Delahaye does furnish some detail, but he is suspect: his book was written years after he was separated from his friend for good, and after he had read Rimbaud's work; there had already been whispers of scandal, and in those days before André Gide's *If It Die* had stirred the mighty chorus of "moi aussi" across Europe, Delahaye's eagerness to testify to Rimbaud's heterosexuality would be understandable. Georges Izambard's contention, to the effect that if indeed there was sexual deviation it was temporary, and to be explained by his old pupil's generally experimental disposition toward life, seems equally inconclusive: he did not see Rimbaud after 1871, and may well be talking about what he would prefer to believe rather than about what he knows.

Attempts to derive a history of Rimbaud's sex life from the

poems are even less satisfactory. He *may*, precociously, have had a mistress. There *may* have been a rupture between them, which *may* have caused a frustration great enough to explain the savagery of "Mes petites amoureuses." But all we know is that he pictures himself with a mistress in "Première soirée," and that the lady he calls Nina is represented as a potential if not an actual sexual partner. Rimbaud's habit of posturing for his own benefit, as well as for his reader, makes it unwise to draw many conclusions.

What we affirm, in spite of our ignorance, is that when Rimbaud pictures felicity some Eros is always at work. It may also be suggested that so long as Rimbaud was in the phase of treating conventional subjects, what love meant to him as an individual was not really an issue, since the poets he knew were not given to praising variations from the sexual norm. In later poems, after the poet had entered the Cities of the Plain without peradventure of doubt, the element of love in the formula of felicity will become vastly more complex, especially since it mixes with his politics in a Whitmanesque desire to embrace large portions of humanity in the mass—and becomes hypostasized as "the New Harmony." But it will never disappear.

Freedom is no less important to him. If the speaker in "Sensation" is "happy as if with a woman," it is not only because he is in the midst of nature but also because he is going where he wishes—if only he can determine where he wants to go. He will, in any case, go far away, and there will be no more restraint upon him than upon a gypsy. His delight may be the kind that Irving Babbitt used to condemn as evidence of Romantic irresponsibility, but his poem has all the charm of the poetry of departing trains and steamers, and of songs of the open road.

Yet this element in Rimbaud's formula of felicity is the least constantly evident of the three. It plays no visible role in either *Une Saison en enfer* or the *Illuminations*. Although obviously a powerful source of feeling through the first years of Rimbaud's poetic career, and an underlying subject of both the "Lettre du voyant" and "Le Bateau ivre," subsequently it drops from sight. One might be tempted to relegate it to a minor place among the drives that move Rimbaud's imagination.

One would be wrong to do so. We should not neglect the fact that in "Première soirée" the speaker is at liberty to entertain an undressed woman in his room, and that the day in the country with Nina involves freedom to go wherever they like; we may also note that the dream of bliss collapses when she reveals that she is not free to leave her office job. Freedom, although not the poet's in this case, is also an issue in "Le Forgeron." And finally, in "Ophélie," it turns out to have had a part in the death of one of Shakespeare's heroines.

4

One could be tempted to neglect these early poems because they are such palpable attempts to perform in the Parnassian manner. To do so, however, would be to neglect the element in them which is permanently characteristic of Rimbaud.

The first of the three parts of "Ophélie" is, indeed, little more than a demonstration of competence, but the second reveals him calling on his total stock of poetic resources.

O pâle Ophélia! belle comme la neige!
Oui, tu mourus, enfant, par un fleuve emporté!
– C'est que les vents tombant des grands monts de Norwège
T'avaient parlé tout bas de l'âpre liberté;

C'est qu'un souffle, tordant ta grande chevelure,
A ton esprit rêveur portait d'étranges bruits;
Que ton cœur écoutait le chant de la Nature
Dans les plaintes de l'arbre et les soupirs des nuits;

C'est que la voix des mers folles, immense râle,
Brisait ton sein d'enfant, trop humain et trop doux;
C'est qu'un matin d'avril, un beau cavalier pâle,
Un pauvre fou, s'assit muet à tes genoux!

Ciel! Amour! Liberté! Quel rêve, ô pauvre Folle!
Tu te fondais à lui comme une neige au feu;
Tes grandes visions étranglaient ta parole
– Et l'Infini terrible effara ton œil bleu!

The first part is a picture of the maiden sliding endlessly down the current. Now the poet intervenes with an apostrophe on the causes of her death. She has died of having harkened to the wind from the Norwegian mountains. (Rimbaud's geography here may seem tortuous, but surely winds blowing over Denmark may originate further north.) To the reader who remembers his *Hamlet*, this is already taking liberties with the libretto. It appears, also, that the wind has been speaking of liberty – and here Rimbaud abandons Shakespeare entirely, since the Ophelia of the play dies not at all from intimations of freedom but as an indirect result of inexorable political necessity. Rimbaud has made some of her misfortune come from listening to nature – the complaints of the forest, the sighing of the night, the voices of the mad sea – as well as from love of the pale, distraught prince. In short, Ophelia's death is here attributed to the experience of the three elements in Rimbaud's formula of felicity and here, as in "Sensation," the experience is productive of dream.

This linking of nature, love, and liberty with a dream is richly suggestive. Explicitly or implicitly, the subject of dreaming comes up with respect not only to this poem but also to all those written up to this time in which the poet purports to be speaking of himself. "Sensation," for example, does not celebrate an actual, present experience but a future and potential one. When summer shall have come (the poem was written in March) the poet will go out in the open country and there be happy. His joy is taken in advance of the event, in a promise that may someday be fulfilled. And, since he says he will then capture a dream, all this is tantamount to saying that he is dreaming at the moment of writing about a dream he will enjoy in the future.

Similarly, although dreaming is not mentioned, or even suggested, in the text of "Première soirée," this poem sounds like a textbook case of adolescent wish fulfillment.

— Elle était fort déshabillée
Et de grands arbres indiscrets
Aux vitres jetaient leur feuillée
Malinement, tout près, tout près.

Assise sur ma grande chaise,
Mi-nue, elle joignait les mains.
Sur le plancher frissonnaient d'aise
Ses petits pieds si fins, si fins.

. . . .

Les petits pieds sous la chemise
Se sauvèrent: «Veux-tu finir!»
— La première audace permise,
Le rire feignait de punir!

— Pauvrets palpitants sous ma lèvre,
Je baisai doucement ses yeux:
— Elle jeta sa tête mièvre
En arrière: «Oh! c'est encor mieux! . . .

The use of personifying qualifiers like "indiscret" and "malinement," the repetitions in the final lines of the first and second stanzas (as well as of the final one, which is not quoted here), the lilting rhythm of the octosyllables, combine to leave an impression of coyness and contrivance; the gaiety of the piece is too carefully planned, the subject matter somewhat too redolent of a kind of pseudo–eighteenth century, and the salient features of the amiably meretricious partner are too unmistakably traditional. One would like, realizing the nature of the poem and feeling it unpleasantly inferior to Rimbaud's other early efforts, to take it for a parody of some of the cloying poetry prevalent at the time; and it is true that one cannot read the piece without wondering whether, even in the remoteness of Charleville, Rimbaud had not heard rumors of a minor revival of the rococco. But unless one is persuaded in advance that he was incapable of writing a weak poem, his having fallen into a very minor mode does not of itself mean parody. It seems more likely that the proper word would be, not parody, but the familiar one, performance: if this was one of the ways poets behaved, he could show himself no less capable of it than the others.

Reducing the poem to prose paraphrase makes it emerge as a kind of pseudo-confession, half-boasting and not expecting to be believed, such as is familiar in the recreation areas of lycées. In other words, this is another phantasy, composed of the usual materials. But this time their importance in relation to each other is reversed. Nature is present, but only in the role of an accomplice. Liberty is present also, as has been mentioned earlier, but both are subordinated to the erotic. Rimbaud's imagination is sporting, if not wallowing, in carnality. I would hesitate to attribute to onanism the role some think it to have had, but would not deny that poems like this one add credibility to the notion of poetry accompanying masturbation. The least to be said is that, parody or no parody, and onanism or no onanism, the young poet is here enjoying the flesh as he is unlikely to have enjoyed it in reality.

Phantasy and wish fulfillment would seem to play an even

more striking role in the bucolic "Réparties de Nina." From the opening image, physiologically incongruous but full of vigor, this piece is an elaborately detailed invitation to come into the country and romp. Everything will be unadulterated pleasure; the couple will go where they want and do what they please. And nature will be not only a lovely décor but also a sympathetic accomplice again.

Lui. – Ta poitrine sur ma poitrine,
    Hein? nous irions,
Ayant de l'air plein la narine,
    Aux frais rayons

Du bon matin bleu, qui vous baigne
    Du vin du jour? . . .
Quand tout le bois frissonnant saigne
    Muet d'amour

De chaque branche, gouttes vertes,
    Des bourgeons clairs,
On sent dans les choses ouvertes
    Frémir des chairs:

. . . .

Dix-sept ans! Tu seras heureuse!
    Oh! les grands prés,
La grande campagne amoureuse!
    – Dis, viens plus près! . . .

Everywhere the countryside is pure delight, and moved, itself, by love. And to the enlivened senses the detail of rural life comes through with extreme immediacy, each item standing out sharply in turn. One may doubt that Rimbaud worked very seriously toward technical perfection in this poem, but not that his imagination dwelt lovingly upon every image.

Ça sentira l'étable, pleine
De fumiers chauds,
Pleine d'un lent rhythme d'haleine,
Et de grands dos

Blanchissant sous quelque lumière;
Et, tout là-bas,
Une vache fientera, fière,
A chaque pas. . .

– Les lunettes de la grand'mère
Et son nez long
Dans son missel; le pot de bière
Cerclé de plomb,

Moussant entre les larges pipes
Qui, crânement,
Fument: les effroyables lippes
Qui, tout fumant,

Happent le jambon aux fourchettes
Tant, tant et plus:
Le feu qui claire les couchettes
Et les bahuts.

The reader does not easily forget that this poet was a country boy and descended from a long line of peasants.

Comparison with "Soleil et chair" makes the nature and quality of the phantasy in "Les Réparties de Nina" unmistakable. Both poems celebrate the flesh, and both invoke the parallel between an amiable and fecund nature on one hand and abundant human genitality on the other. But between the two pieces is the distance which separates a poem where the poet is seeing what he feels obligated to see and one in which the vision is deeply private and personal. In his outing with Nina he is so close to his subject that at one point he imagines the luminous glint of the skin of a baby's bottom; in "Soleil et chair" the distance between him and the objects of his contemplation is tremendous. He does not *see* them, perhaps, so much as *refer* to them:

— O Vénus, ô Déesse!
Je regrette les temps de l'antique jeunesse,
Des satyres lascifs, des faunes animaux,
Dieux qui mordaient d'amour l'écorce des rameaux
Et dans les nénufars baisaient la Nymphe blonde!
Je regrette les temps où la sève du monde,
L'eau du fleuve, le sang rose des arbres verts
Dans les veines de Pan mettaient un univers!

Où le sol palpitait, vert, sous ses pieds de chèvre;
Où, baisant mollement le clair syrinx, sa lèvre
Modulait sous le ciel le grand hymne d'amour;
Où, debout sur la plaine, il entendait autour
Répondre à son appel la Nature vivante;
Où les arbres muets, berçant l'oiseau qui chante,
La terre berçant l'homme, et tout l'Océan bleu
Et tous les animaux aimaient, aimaient en Dieu!
Je regrette les temps de la grande Cybèle
Qu'on disait parcourir, gigantesquement belle,
Sur un grand char d'airain, les splendides cités;
Son double sein versait dans les immensités
Le pur ruissellement de la vie infinie.
L'Homme suçait, heureux, sa mamelle bénie,
Comme un petit enfant, jouant sur ses genoux.
— Parce qu'il était fort, l'Homme était chaste et doux.

In one poem he wants only to be a poet; in the other he wants to be in the country with a girl, and the wish is father to proximity, warmth, and authenticity.

5

These considerations, taken together, leave a strong suggestion that in his first phase Rimbaud had already made poetry an escape from real surroundings which he did not find particularly pleasant. There is at least a hint, also, that he suspects the practice of being dangerous: Ophelia is lured to death by the combination of things that make up his dream of felicity. And, moreover, there is an additional hint that he realizes the nature of the ironic contrast between his phantasy and his actual situation: the last stanza of the "Réparties de Nina" runs through a crescendo of excited, broken cries of invitation; then, in the last line, the girl's voice brings everything back to earth: "Et mon bureau?" Despite the plural noun of the title, this reminder that she has a job is her one speech in the poem. Triumphant reality speaks through her. The very object of the phantasy finally destroys it. This is the first appearance of the curious ambivalence which will persist throughout Rimbaud's pursuit of felicity: even in his most excited and abandoned moments a still small voice will warn of the possibilities of failure. The recurrent touch of self-irony will insist that much as he may want to drink the milk of paradise, the chances that he, Jean-Arthur Rimbaud, of Charleville on the Meuse, will ever taste it are rather small.

Our picture of Rimbaud in this phase is in some ways hard to distinguish from that of a typical adolescent with an incipient vocation to poetry. He wants to be a poet and, accordingly, he writes poems, and, since at his age he has few subjects available, he tends to draw heavily on his phantasies. These form an ideal of happiness which is not particularly sharp in outline but is always made of the same stuff—our already familiar triad. He is aware of a certain incongruity between his place in life and the felicity he would like to attain.

We suspect, also, that his phantasy offered him an avenue

of escape from a real life that must have been desperately drab. It is hard to believe that if his mother, Vitalie, had read these poems, she would have been quite so astonished when her younger son began running away from home. But Vitalie Rimbaud was not a woman to read, and learn from, poetry.

Chapter II – The Taste of Freedom

RIMBAUD's first phase ended on August 29, 1870. Here for once we can set an exact date. This was the day when he sold his books and took the train for Paris – where he was picked up for having ridden farther than he had paid to ride. Shortly he was writing his friend Izambard, with urgency, to come and take him out of the Mazas prison. Izambard did so, took the fugitive back to his own home in Douai for rehabilitation, and then returned with him to Charleville and a monumentally displeased mother. What had begun as high adventure ended in ignominy, with Rimbaud promising to amend his life and avoid the further occasion of sin – a promise which was no sooner made than broken.

But if we know when and how all this took place, we surely do not know why, or the reason for its happening when it did.

Was Rimbaud running away from something? In view of his subsequent unhappy relations with his mother it is easy to assume so. Madame Rimbaud seems to have been the kind of mother any son would be tempted to run away from, and whether we judge her fairly or do her the grossest injustice, the fact is that she had consistently bad luck keeping her men folk at home. Her eldest son, a lout named Frédéric, had already taken to the open road, following the example of the father, also named Frédéric, who had abandoned the family to all practical intents years before. Rimbaud's biographers, agreed on so few matters, are unanimous with regard to this one: as wife and mother Vitalie was no great success. No one thinks of her as anything but harsh and unmotherly, despite the testimony of her daughter Isabelle, who has gone down in history as more dutiful than veracious. Yet when one looks for evidence that before his sudden departure Rimbaud had been rebellious, or even restive, there is none. Even Izambard, no admirer of Vitalie, reports that the escapade took her entirely by surprise. Nothing indicates that the boy had found his surroundings intolerable up to that time, however they might affect him during the months to follow. Once he had felt it, the urge to run away seems to have been irresistible: Izambard had hardly turned his back, after bringing him home the first time, before the miscreant was on the road again. But this does not prove that he was trying to leave something *behind* him. There is as good a chance that he was drawn, not driven, away. But by what?

Possibly the promise of excitement in a Paris which had just gone to war would have been enough. But by the testimony of his poems, this was not the only lure. Rimbaud had also seen an opportunity to realize his favorite dream.

For the familiar vision is very much with him. Of the fourteen poems that are attached to this period of the fugues, all but one treat the general subject of felicity. The exception, "Tête de faune," is emotionally neutral. Of the others, seven ("A la musique," "Roman," "Rêve pour l'hiver," "Au cabaret-vert," "Le Buffet," "La Maline," and "Ma bohème") are animated by a feeling of harmony with the universe. Five ("Morts de quatre-vingt-douze," "Le Mal," "Rages de Césars," "Le Dormeur du val," and "L'Eclatante Victoire de Sarrebruck") attack the one thing that intrudes in his universe to spoil his beatitude, the war. And one, "Les Effarés," is about the spectacle of the discomfort, if not specifically of the unhappiness, of someone else.

There is also a striking difference between the poems of this time that talk of his joy and delight and those of his first phase. The earlier ones had dealt with imagined but unexperienced happiness; he is now reporting what he actually knows. Consequently these new pictures of his felicity are extremely personal: whereas the voice that says "je" in the first phase is hardly more than a dramatic convention, and could be that of almost anybody, the one that speaks after the first fugue is clearly his own — that of a personality rather than a persona. Witness, for example, "Roman":

I

On n'est pas sérieux, quand on a dix-sept ans.
— Un beau soir, foin des bocks et de la limonade,
Des cafés tapageurs aux lustres éclatants!
— On va sous les tilleuls verts de la promenade.

Les tilleuls sentent bon dans les bons soirs de juin!
L'air est parfois si doux, qu'on ferme la paupière;
Le vent chargé de bruits, — la ville n'est pas loin, —
A des parfums de vigne et des parfums de bière . . .

II

— Voilà qu'on aperçoit un tout petit chiffon

D'azur sombre, encadré d'une petite branche,
Piqué d'une mauvaise étoile, qui se fond
Avec de doux frissons, petite et toute blanche . . .

Nuit de juin! Dix-sept ans! – On se laisse griser.
La sève est du champagne et vous monte à la tête . . .
On divague; on se sent aux lèvres un baiser
Qui palpite là, comme une petite bête . . .

III

Le cœur fou Robinsonne à travers les romans,
– Lorsque, dans la clarté d'un pâle réverbère,
Passe une demoiselle aux petits airs charmants,
Sous l'ombre du faux-col effrayant de son père . . .

Et, comme elle vous trouve immensément naïf,
Tout en faisant trotter ses petites bottines,
Elle se tourne, alerte et d'un mouvement vif . . .
– Sur vos lèvres alors meurent les cavatines . . .

IV

Vous êtes amoureux. Loué jusqu'au mois d'août.
Vous êtes amoureux. – Vos sonnets La font rire.
Tous vos amis s'en vont, vous êtes mauvais goût.
– Puis l'adorée, un soir, a daigné vous écrire! . . .

– Ce soir-là . . . – vous rentrez aux cafés éclatants,
Vous demandez des bocks ou de la limonade . . .
– On n'est pas sérieux, quand on a dix-sept ans
Et qu'on a des tilleuls verts sur la promenade.

In these familiar verses, which appear inevitably in the anthologies, phantasy is replaced by the solidity of fact. And this is equally true of "Ma bohème," in which appears, as is rarely the case elsewhere, an entirely attractive Rimbaud.

Je m'en allais, les poings dans mes poches crevées;
Mon paletot aussi devenait idéal;
J'allais sous le ciel, Muse! et j'étais ton féal;
Oh! là là! que d'amours splendides j'ai rêvées!

Mon unique culotte avait un large trou.
— Petit-Poucet rêveur, j'égrenais dans ma course
Des rimes. Mon auberge était à la Grande-Ourse.
— Mes étoiles au ciel avaient un doux frou-frou.

Et je les écoutais, assis au bord des routes,
Ces bons soirs de septembre où je sentais des gouttes
De rosée à mon front, comme un vin de vigueur;

Où, rimant au milieu des ombres fantastiques,
Comme des lyres, je tirais les élastiques
De mes souliers blessés, un pied près de mon cœur!

In poems like these the scenes of the experiences are now specified. "A la musique" is set in the Place de la Gare, Charleville. The inn of "Au cabaret-vert" is on the outskirts of Charleroi, in Belgium. So is the restaurant in "La Maline." Although the actual location of "Le Buffet" is not stated, the factual detail of the poem — furniture, color, and smells — leave the conviction that Rimbaud has been physically present in the room he describes. The road he is following in "Ma bohème" is not named, but we know that it can only be the one leading away from Charleville into Belgium and eventually on back to Douai.

His time perspective has shifted accordingly. Only one of the new poems, "Rêve pour l'hiver," goes off into the familiarly indefinite future of phantasy, and its effect is to remind us how complete the absence of such indefiniteness is in the rest. In these others he has abandoned the verbal tense structure that goes with the anticipation of enjoyment in favor either of a past so close to the present as to be almost indistinguishable from it—as in "A la musique"—or of a present which makes the reader witness of the event, or else, for example in "Au cabaret-vert," a past to be contemplated with retrospective pleasure and, perhaps, even recaptured.

In the circumstances one is not surprised to find him considerably more aware of himself. It is a fine thing to be off, like a gypsy, tramping along with the whole universe at concert pitch, but tramping wears out one's shoes and an overcoat too long worn becomes less a garment than the Platonic Ideal of one. Following after the girls through the park on a sweet evening is a rare pleasure, but this does not alter the fact of his clothes being as sloppy "as a student's." And the self-irony which earlier took shape in the sudden deflation of his plans for a romp with Nina now makes him remember that he is small enough to be something of a Tom Thumb, and that, in the grip of intense puppy love, he must look funny. The distinction between dream and reality is clear.

The closeness of his contact with reality even extends to sex. Except in "Rêve pour l'hiver," in which there is an abundance of wish fulfillment, he recognizes his desires for what they are: imaginary gratification is replaced by an image of himself wanting to be, but not being, gratified. There are girls about, and, out by himself in the fresh spring evening, he feels as if he has just been kissed on the mouth or else is about to be—and the kiss is not innocent. Nor is it borrowed from a Watteauesque eighteenth century which never was on land or sea.

Admittedly, his notion of euphoria at this moment is not a particularly sophisticated one. He sounds a bit like Jean-Jacques Rousseau spending the day in the country with the young Misses Gaffenried—a day highlighted by Rousseau's tossing down cherries from the top of the tree into the receptive bosoms of the young ladies. But Rimbaud, young as he is, has the advantage of Rousseau to the extent that he is somewhat more aware of the meaning of his behavior. The self-portrait at the end of "A la musique" is categorical in this respect.

> Je ne dis pas un mot: je regarde toujours
> La chair de leurs cous blancs brodés de mèches folles:
> Je suis, sous le corsage et les frêles atours,
> Le dos divin après la courbe des épaules.
>
> J'ai bientôt déniché la bottine, le bas . . .
> — Je reconstruis les corps, brûlé de belles fièvres.
> Elles me trouvent drôle et se parlent tout bas . . .
> — Et mes désirs brutaux s'accrochent à leurs lèvres . . .

The last line was too explicit for Izambard, who read the poem and "gave" his pupil a verse from one of his own poems to replace what offended him. The incident makes one interrogative about the ultimate value of Izambard's influence, but it has the merit of calling attention to the tone of self-revelation in Rimbaud's line. Izambard does not appear in his writings to have been at all prudish, but he was a conformist, and the canons of the time favored the impersonal; it was not good to talk of one's private impulses.

But Rimbaud does talk about them, and in so doing gives the measure of his own maturity. So does his disposition toward himself in "Roman," which is not only lovely and gay, but also a deeply comic poem. The poet is not only the actor in the piece; he is audience also, and one which recognizes itself as such. In the opening half he disparages himself by using the impersonal "on," which refers to him as one would refer to an amusing child. Then, in the second half, he shifts to the second person, more definite, "vous." The girl in the poem, whom the "vous" is following, finds *you* very naïve, *you* gather. And when she turns around, the song *you* are singing dies on *your* lips.

Michel Butor has recently caused a considerable stir in France by using a similar *vous* to represent the hero of a novel in which the discourse is entirely internal. The word implies for Butor, as it did for Rimbaud, that the hero is remarkably like everyone else, identifying him with the anonymous general run of men. But at the same time it takes over the work done in normal syntax by the first person, with an implication that might be expressed by some formula like: "I, seeing myself as other men must see me, address myself to you, who are like me." Butor's experiment may be used as a comment on Rimbaud's practice. The ability to see himself from a certain distance, unexpected in an individual so self-centered as Rimbaud clearly was, reminds us that shortly after this he would write, in the "Lettre du voyant," his most often quoted phrase, "JE est un autre." His gift for seeing himself as if he were someone else seems to have been useful, first of all, in preserving him from self-deception.

Though wish fulfillment now appears to be forsaken, dreaming of another kind is not. Months before, in "Sensation," he had hinted at an identification between happiness and what he then called, simply, *rêve*: "Rêveur, je sentirai la fraîcheur à mes pieds." Now, in "Ma bohème," he carries the identification further: the dream is of splendid loves and the dream *is* poetry. Twice in this poem he links the two ideas, and from his insistence we get a first inkling of something which will be useful in reading "Le Bateau ivre": euphoria, dream, and poetry are inseparable.

But we risk misunderstanding the role of dream—and of wish fulfillment also—if we do not emphasize that he is a poet with his feet firmly planted. One of the changes in his vocabulary is symptomatic, perhaps especially because connected with his eroticism: for the "sein" of the earlier period he now uses "téton."

2

Such is his happiness in the second phase of his career. All the senses are keenly, almost painfully, awake and nature shares his mood. The weather is always fair, the natural world is good, joyous, even holy. Freedom is absolute—when he has it. But he also has cause to notice that freedom, and felicity, are exceedingly transitory.

Three times between August 1870 and March 1871 he tried to make good his escape from Charleville. There may even have been a fourth attempt (May 1871). Each was a lesson in how such bids for happiness end. One sets out in joy, but the open road leads nowhere in especial and one has no money; one asks for help and the price of help is the eventual surrender of liberty. From the second fugue he is brought back across country, passed along toward home from the hand of one rural policeman to another. From the third he returns alone, voluntarily, too hungry to stay away. There can have been little poetry in such ignominy, and even less in the prospect of facing the wrath of Vitalie Cuif Rimbaud. And yet happiness was inextricable from this experience which he must have recognized as being doomed from the start—if not when he first ran away, at least after the second attempt. Able to see himself with some detachment, as we know he was, he cannot have failed to see in such bids for felicity the outlines of an eternally defeated purpose.

Yet to judge by the poems, he was less disturbed by this possibility of failure than by the more immediate obstacle to happiness—the war. In the economy of Rimbaud's universe, nature is holy, and war is desecration. The mangled dead in the open fields are tragically out of place, cosmically wrong. This is the obverse of the medal whose face is felicity.

Neglect of this can lead to misreading "Le Dormeur du val":

C'est un trou de verdure où chante une rivière
Accrochant follement aux herbes des haillons
D'argent; où le soleil, de la montagne fière,
Luit: c'est un petit val qui mousse de rayons.

Un soldat jeune, bouche ouvert, tête nue,
Et la nuque baignant dans le frais cresson bleu,
Dort; il est étendu dans l'herbe, sous la nue,
Pâle dans son lit vert où la lumière pleut.

Les pieds dans les glaïeuls, il dort. Souriant comme
Sourirait un enfant malade, il fait un somme:
Nature, berce-le chaudement: il a froid.

Les parfums ne font pas frissonner sa narine;
Il dort dans le soleil, la main sur sa poitrine
Tranquille. Il a deux trous rouges au côté droit.

This poem is not necessarily one of Rimbaud's best, even though it is included in practically every collection of nineteenth-century poetry. Undoubtedly the sudden revelation of the two red holes in the right side of the sleeping soldier is melodramatic and a bit adolescent; there may also be something if not false at least suspiciously arch in the apostrophe of the first tercet: "Nature, berce-le chaudement: il a froid." But granting that this is one of the most self-conscious of the poems of Rimbaud's second phase, and the most reminiscent of the earlier ones in which he was so busy proving to himself that he was a poet, it is still good enough for the reader to be obligated to approach it properly, avoiding the a priori assumption that Rimbaud is not emotionally involved. He has not placed himself at a "Parnassian" distance from his subject.

Reading "Le Dormeur du val" as a "Parnassian" piece is possible only if one lifts it completely out of the context of the other poems written in the autumn of 1870, and if one also forgets how much nature meant to Rimbaud as one of the essential keys to human felicity. The imagery of the piece tells its own story: there is the little valley, the "hole of green," and the small stream singing along as its spray hangs rags of silver on the overhanging grass; the scene bathes in sunshine until the valley bubbles with light; the cress is blue; there is wild flag growing; the grass makes a green bed and the liquid light rains upon it; and the whole scene is so scented that any man's nostrils would tremble. As a picture of nature at her smiling finest it would be hard to find anything wrong here. The tone is right; the vision is an early example of the natural "impressionism" toward which Rimbaud's maturing eye had begun to move. But upon this perfect scene intrudes the figure of the soldier, hatless, his head in the cress and his feet in the wild flags, smiling like a child, seemingly asleep and really dead. The parts of the poem having to do with him are the awkward ones, stiff, off-tone (almost cloying: "berce-le . . ."), immature. This contrast should be taken into account for the final judgment. To take the poem as a completely self-contained work, and a fully realized one, is to risk falling into the error of finding the dominant mood to be ironic, the disposition of the poet to be an ironic detachment.

The curious contrast in the quality of the images here rarely gets the attention it deserves. Everything in normal association with nature is treated "impressionistically." The main effect, in the rendering of the setting, is produced by an enumeration of nouns which move the eye from wide to narrow focus: the green "trou," the river at its bottom, the grass along the bank, the flash of light off the moisture on the damp grass. The main work done by the verbs, meanwhile, is largely the creation of a feeling about the scene, through metaphor: the river "sings," and "hangs" rags of silver, while the sun makes the little valley "bubble" with light. Obviously a metaphor like "bubble" tells the reader little enough about the valley and how it looks; no more does a metaphor like the one in the eighth line which makes the light "rain." But they do tell him an immense amount about how the poet feels the scene.

In contrast, everything connected with the dead soldier is rendered with an objectivity that is entirely "naturalistic." The dominant metaphor, which equates death with sleep, is less a true metaphor than one of the eternal *topoi*. The technique is straightforwardly descriptive: the soldier sleeps, his head here, his feet there; he is pale; he smiles, and so forth; there are the two holes. The clash of the presence of the corpse in an otherwise idyllic scene is repeated in the clash of the two styles, and, in turn, asserts the clash between nature, which is good, and war, which is evil. War defiles nature, as it denies freedom and negates love.

From the beginning there have been hints in Rimbaud's poetry that he cares less for describing nature than for suggesting the feeling she arouses in him. Now, in the autumn of 1870, this tendency becomes more marked. The reader still knows what aspect of nature, what detail, is behind the feeling, just as he sees in Manet's paintings the outlines of the cathedral off which the light is reflected, but Rimbaud has already reached the point where he does not hesitate to take nature to pieces and restore her in a different shape if doing so renders his feeling better. Lines like: "Mes étoiles au ciel avaient un doux frou-frou" ("Ma bohème") and "une mauvaise étoile qui se fond Avec de doux frissons, petite et toute blanche" ("Roman"), are surely more intent on conveying emotion than on astronomical accuracy. Nature is simply forced to submit to the poet's purpose.

In "Tête de faune" the situation is not quite one of taking nature to pieces, but is perhaps even more significant: the eye hardly succeeds in getting through the flashing light to the nature behind it. There are no woods, but only leaves and flowers. Of the faun himself we see nothing but the eyes, and the white of the teeth which bite red flowers; after his departure his laughter stays behind him on the trembling leaves. It is as if the poet were too delighted to make the effort to see; the retina would seem to be a passively receptive instrument, out of direct contact with the corresponding areas of the brain. The feeling of rational quiescence is strengthened when "le baiser dort" of the third line, where the kiss sleeps on the shining flowers, becomes "le baiser d'or" of the last. Under analysis, this word play does not quite turn out to be a Joycean pun, but readers of *Finnegans Wake* will recognize the irrational though meaningful transfer. The appeal of "Tête de faune" lies in its almost delirious immediacy. But we are occupied here less with the passing appeal of one poem than with the incipience of a habit of Rimbaud's imagination which will become pivotal, in later phases, for the understanding of his poetry. Attentive readers of this poem, of "Le Dormeur du val," of "Roman" and "Ma bohème," will not be particularly surprised when, in the poems written in 1872, the landscape of which the poet speaks constantly becomes a private one to which he does not trouble to admit us.

Felicity was fragile. Freedom could be, and was, easily denied. For all Rimbaud's attempts to escape, he spent most of the winter of 1870–1871 in Charleville, with no choice but obey a mother whom he had come to dislike, surrounded by people from whom he was alienated, forced to go to a church he despised because it was the ally of his intimate enemies. His friends had left because of the war. Everything was out of joint and he had no way to set it right.

His one weapon of retaliation was a private one. Already during his second phase he had castigated some of the sponsors of the war, discovering that poetry can be used to express one's aggressions and thus, presumably, relieve them. Such poems are the forerunners of the whole series in which he lashes out at everything and everyone he dislikes.

If he could not be happy he could at least be horrid.

Chapter III – Winter of His Discontent

BAD TEMPER now becomes a major factor in Rimbaud's development. His letters and the testimony of his friends bear out the conclusion to be drawn from the poems themselves: woe betide whoever or whatever crossed him. His capacity for resentment was deep.

So was his capacity for expressing it, and since the resentment rose from personal frustration his expression becomes increasingly personal also. The poems of late 1870 in which he vents his spleen at the people and things standing between him and what he wants are those in which his individuality is most completely and authentically confirmed. Displeasure gives him a pitiless eye and sharpens his tongue.

Even earlier, in "Vénus anadyomène," there had been at least a hint that his talent might develop in this direction. A woman, with the words "Clara Vénus" inscribed across the small of her back, heaves her telluric bulk up out of the bath:

> Puis le col gras et gris, les larges omoplates
> Qui saillent; le dos court qui rentre et qui ressort;
> Puis les rondeurs des reins semblent prendre l'essor;
> La graisse sous la peau paraît en feuilles plates . . .

The more of her there is to see, the less attractive the effect, and the last line reveals that she suffers from an anal ulcer. Venus indeed! The irony is too broad to want, or permit, comment; the only question is why Rimbaud should have written anything so out of key with the rest of what he was writing at the time.

He may have been replying to a dizain by François Coppée in the *Parnasse Contemporain* which twitted young poets for not knowing what women really look like. But it is not certain that Rimbaud had read Coppée's piece, and another hypothesis presents itself. "Vénus anadyomène" must have been written a relatively short time after "Soleil et chair," his Parnassian salute to the ancient Golden Age. "I believe in you," he had cried with more rhetorical abundance than fervor, "I believe in you, Divine Mother, Aphrodite of the Sea!" The verb "believe" is variable as to content in such contexts: it has very little in this one and small claim to be taken seriously. There is every reason to doubt that the Dawn of the World, which he sees through such correctly Parnassian eyes, was very real to Rimbaud. Probably his real meaning is that almost any world, ancient or imaginary, would be preferable to the outrageously defective one he found about him. "Vénus anadyomène" thus makes excellent sense as a coda to "Soleil et chair." If the myth of a lovely and more fecund life can be subsumed in the figure of a perfect goddess, the sad sterility and ugliness of life in the modern world can find its fitting emblem in the figure of a fat lady with a sore bottom.

This is the first opportunity we have had to observe Rimbaud in an act of rejection. There will be numerous others where what he is doing will be more clearly apparent, but now is as good a time as any to note that his rejections are invariably performed in the name of some criterion: the refusal of adult life in *Une Saison en enfer* asserts the value of some lost innocence of childhood, and that of life in Europe the existence of an Orient which has no discoverable place in geography. We should notice now, as will be necessary again later, that the criteria in question are negative: they correspond not to something but to the *absence* of something; they put flesh upon an awareness of what his life fails to provide. Surely if, in the depths of a New England winter, one expresses an intention of going to live, say, in the Dry Tortugas, one can hardly be held at a subsequent time to have preferred life on some sterile tropical island; what the remark reveals is, rather, a particular disposition toward New England in January.

There is no need, consequently, to think that Rimbaud subscribed literally to the neopagan myth of the Parnassians. The attitude he expresses is focused upon life in the French provinces in 1870. One may have no belief in a past which, however pleasantly pictured, has the defect of never having existed, and still make the image of it an excellent bludgeon with which to assault one's own time.

This consideration bears in turn upon one of the subjects by which recent criticism has been most fascinated. The word Revolt itself has acquired strong metaphysical resonances which, no doubt, are come by honestly in the cases of writers like Camus and Malraux. Rimbaud's qualifications for dealing with metaphysics have, however, never been demonstrated. Whatever he rejects, his reasons for the rejection, so far as they can be discovered at all, turn out to be private, instinctive, and most unsystematic. Of course, if Camus is correct in defining the *révolté* as a man capable of pronouncing an absolute No—if this is indeed all it takes—and if the present reading of "Vénus anadyomène" is correct, we have found an act of revolt in a poem belonging to Rimbaud's first phase. As we follow him through the winter of his confinement in Charleville, he will repeat it often, more explicitly, and with greater violence. But at no point will he attempt a philosophical justification of his sense of outrage.

But if "Vénus anadyomène" is an act of refusal it is also an act of aggression, and its manner is thus as important for us as its matter. One would be hard put to name another poet since Swift who has wallowed so willingly in the disgusting. Swift may even be the less relentless of the two, since his rhyme does admit a certain cloacal humor. Rimbaud never lets us take our eye off what he wants us to see, and the worst is reserved for the final line.

Now one does not write smut on the walls of privies one knows to be unfrequented; obscene performances posit an audience and obscene writings, a reader. If, as I am suggesting, "Vénus anadyomène" is an act of protest, and of aggression against the modern world, it is also one against any reader who is in any way partisan of the world Rimbaud rejects.

Before the winter of 1870–1871 is out, the poet will be going around inscribing blasphemies like "Merde à Dieu" in public places. Such conduct has been taken to be a symptom of rebellion against religion. This interpretation is an error founded on a basic ignorance of the ways of adolescents. The hope of putting the Deity in a state of outrage is small and remote, at least as compared with the richer possibilities of enraging some adherent of the Deity who is close at hand. One's mother, her fellow members of the middle class, the parish priest, are far likelier material. The real object of aggression in "Vénus anadyomène" and similar poems must be assumed to be immediately present, in Charleville. Readers who, a century later, tend naturally to identify themselves with the poet, miss some of the sting of his wrath; they should try, once at least, to identify with his targets—among which they would doubtless have found themselves had they lived in the right time and place.

Probably Rimbaud's impact is so great because he goes so coolly about his task. Each detail is in place and there is no blur. One feels not only that the stream is being polluted but that the polluting is entirely intentional. When he attacks the things he loathes, the poet's syntax remains lucidly and complexly organized, and his vision is unaffected by what has been called the "impressionism" which has already been seen in his poems about felicity. We have found these two types of vision dramatized, in a dialectic relation to each other, in "Le Dormeur du val." Of the two kinds, it is the literal, "naturalistic" one—quite as severely attentive to the exterior world as the vision of any of the novelists who will shortly cluster around Emile Zola—which will predominate through the long, crucial winter.

Anger is not, however, the sole determining factor, and perhaps not always the decisive one. It seems, rather, that what incites Rimbaud to see reality with such a puritanically clear eye is the spectacle of unhappiness. When the unhappiness is his own, and pity transforms itself into self-pity, anger stirs also and he can be savage; but in certain poems where his own welfare is not involved his sight is as clear as in poems obviously written in wrath. Thus, already, "Les Effarés":

> Noirs dans la neige et dans la brume,
> Au grand soupirail qui s'allume,
> Leurs culs en rond,

A genoux, cinq petits – misère! –
Regardent le Boulanger faire
    Le lourd pain blond.

Ils voient le fort bras blanc qui tourne
La pâte grise et qui l'enfourne
    Dans un trou clair.

Ils écoutent le bon pain cuire.
Le Boulanger au gras sourire
    Grogne un vieil air.

Ils sont blottis, pas un ne bouge,
Au souffle du soupirail rouge
    Chaud comme un sein.

. . . .

Ils se ressentent si bien vivre,
Les pauvres Jésus pleins de givre,
    Qu'ils sont là tous,

Collant leurs petits museaux roses
Au treillage, grognant des choses
    Entre les trous,

Si fort, qu'ils crèvent leur culotte
Et que leur chemise tremblote
    Au vent d'hiver.

This poem about some cold and hungry children, so beside themselves with excitement as they squat to watch the hot loaves come out of the oven that they are unconscious of straining their clothes beyond the breaking point, is a parade of visual images. The perspective moves unobtrusively from what the observer sees of the group back-to him outside the baker's window, to what the children see inside, thence to the observer again. The last five stanzas do double duty in that they continue the description and at the same time suggest the effect of the experience upon the children. The emotion affirmed in the poet's cry, "misère," in a few interpolated adjectives, and in the appositive "pauvres Jésus pleins de givre" is otherwise allowed to develop out of the description. The syntax is excellent confirmation of what has been reported here about Rimbaud's linguistic behavior in such poems: it is extremely firm. The whole syntactical structure consists of five declarative sentences of six, three, three, three, and twenty-one verses respectively, with the last sentence consisting of three adverbial time clauses, a main clause, a clause in apposition to the subject of the main clause, a result clause accompanied by its own descriptive appositions, and finally an adverbial clause. The relations between these parts admit no ambiguity: as a statement, this poem is as clear as a lawyer's brief, and completely undisturbed by the emotion which even so infuses the whole piece.

Cecil A. Hackett's psychoanalysis of this piece in *Rimbaud l'enfant* is brilliant, but because of its very brilliance may divert the attention of the reader from an essential fact: even if equating this oven with the womb and the loaves with the new born is full of exciting possibilities, the overt meaning of the poem is completely adequate already. This is not a phantasy like "Fêtes de la faim," in which Rimbaud's appetite for stones cries aloud for psychoanalytic interpretation. "Les Effarés" may indeed be analyzed if one insists on doing so, but the essential aspects of the poem—its wholeness, the completeness with which the idea is worked out, its syntactical solidity—are in danger of being overlooked.

The psychiatric analysis would be particularly regrettable if it resulted in our losing sight of the nature of Rimbaud's vision in this piece, which is attentive to the world outside the author's mind in the way a scene from Flaubert would be, and as untroubled and as coherent. We should not be diverted, either, from the fact that this detachment is unmixed with any intention of shocking the reader. No aggression is involved. As in "Le Dormeur du val," Rimbaud's preoccupation with his private beatitude does not intrude. There will not be many such poems among those written during this winter. We shall need a clear view of those we have in order to understand the others, where his own felicity is at issue.

2

Rimbaud's disposition toward the war was necessarily complex. In "Le Dormeur du val," war had borne responsibility for the one false note which ruined the idyllic harmony of nature. Yet it also offered a promise of action and excitement. During his second fugue he was eager to enlist in the Home Guards of Douai, and later, during the Commune, he was again moved to take a part in the fighting. Laugh as he would at the bourgeois in their overstuffed uniforms, we know that he had moments of wanting to defend his country against the invader or to take up arms in defense of his republican principles. But he was too young, and too small, to lie successfully about his age. Here was a source of additional frustration.

Everything conspired to teach him a lesson he was in no way eager to learn — that his place was at home with the mother who was also his custodian. The war even inhibited movement and in this way, too, was a radical infringement of freedom. Hostile armies in the field, simply by existing, obstruct the open road; they were one more reason for his mother's keeping him under her thumb.

Nothing, however, justifies the assumption that all Rimbaud's objections to war were private and personal. He appears also to have felt a moral revulsion untinged by personal interest. The sonnet called "Le Mal" dwells not on personal inconvenience or its intrusions upon nature, but upon the killing of so many men and the causing of so much sorrow that compassion stirs even in a God whom Rimbaud conceives as ordinarily indifferent to humanity.

If war is thus hateful, so are its authors. At this point his politics and his humanitarianism stand together. He is too much a republican not to detest Napoleon III. The Emperor of "Rages de Césars" is the same monarch who in "Le Mal" laughs as men go to their death. This enemy of liberty is still drunk after twenty years of power. It is good that things no longer go well for him. "Rages de Césars" and "Le Mal" are hate poetry. And another sonnet, "L'Eclatante Victoire de Sarrebruck," pictures the Emperor:

> . . . raide, sur son dada
> Flamboyant; très heureux, — car il voit tout en rose,
> Féroce comme Zeus et doux comme un papa . . .

The piece goes on to paint a scene in which, when one soldier cries "Vive l'Empereur," another, who has been lying on his belly, heaves himself up from the ground backside first, shouting: "What for?"

In "Morts de quatre-vingt-douze," the supporters of Emperor and war fare hardly better than the victims of Victor Hugo's *Châtiments*. A political hack named Cassagnac, one of a father and son team who worked for *Le Pays*, writing in that paper, had urged Frenchmen of all political nuances to rally to the national cause, remembering the example of the men of the Revolution. From such antirepublicans the appeal might have seemed less than sincere to any reader; to Rimbaud it was scandalous.

> Vous dont le sang lavait toute grandeur salie,
> Morts de Valmy, Morts de Fleurus, Morts d'Italie,
> O million de Christs aux yeux sombres et doux;

Nous vous laissions dormir avec la République,
Nous, courbés sous les rois comme sous une trique.
— Messieurs de Cassagnac nous reparlent de vous!

In "Chant de guerre parisien," even the statesman Thiers, who had opposed the war in the beginning, joins the enemies of liberty and bears with them a scorn so deep that, to express it, Rimbaud descends to pun: "Thiers et Picard sont des Eros."

That the poetry he wrote about the war and politics is relatively thin stuff illustrates the rule that Rimbaud's intensity diminishes with the distance of the subject. A tension created by the juxtaposition of two manners in one poem, as in "Le Dormeur du val," or an irony which depends for existence upon remaining inexplicit, appear sufficient to express his feeling. Possibly his attitudes depend too much on theory. In any event, to judge by the poems themselves, he is more likely to extend his powers, at this stage in his development, when what offends him is more immediately at hand—his mother, his mother's church, the librarians who are reluctant to give him the books he wants to read, and the people of Charleville, those *Lumpenbourgeois.* To be his bitterest he needs his subjects to be nearby.

3

Obviously the child pictured in "Les Poètes de sept ans" is wretched; he fears his mother and detests her; the absence of instinctive sympathy between them is fundamental. She commands obedience and he obeys, and doing so makes him a hypocrite. But when she catches him in the wrong and he heaps affection on her because he can see how disturbed she is, her response is equally hypocritical. His getting caught seems to have involved playing with the wrong children—but there are no others to play with. And Sundays, when he is compelled to dress up, slick his hair, and read the Bible, are the abomination of desolation.

How good is Rimbaud's memory and how accurate his report? When we consider that at this time he is referring to his mother in his letters to Izambard as "la bouche d'ombre," and complaining that she is the source of his current unhappiness because she has shut off his pocket money in revenge for his running away from home, we may well begin to wonder. He is so alienated from Vitalie that his testimony may be accepted only as that of a hostile witness. What is clear is that now, before his eighteenth birthday, he has no use for her. It is less clear that he had felt the same ten years earlier.

The factual background of the piece may be correct. It is not hard to believe that Madame Rimbaud stood over her children while they did their lessons, that her concern for respectability made her refuse to let them play with the neglected ragamuffins down the block, or even that she made Sundays unbearable for one and all. One is less disposed to take what the poem reports about the boy's emotions at face value. At the age of seven was he so committed to sentimental republicanism that he was aware of loving God the less and man the more? Did he really make up stories in which the word liberty was so important as to require a capital? Had he already, *at seven,* formed his notion of felicity?

> — Il rêvait la prairie amoureuse, où des houles
> Lumineuses, parfums sains, pubescences d'or,
> Font leur remuement calme et prennent leur essor!

He says such things in the poem, and we know that he was precocious, but there are limits even for Rimbaud. It seems prudent to consider "Les Poètes de sept ans" another instance of the rule that the rebellious adolescent searches the past for evidence that his parents have reared him faultily.

The references at the beginning of *Une Saison en enfer* to some state of juvenile grace, untroubled and uncorrupted, and greatly preferable to his later moral condition, hardly bear out this other report of his childhood. The child who appears here does not sound a bit more innocent than the average run of little boys—if as much. All in all, a cautious reader will prefer to read "Les Poètes de sept ans" as an aggression against his mother, who in 1870–1871 stood in the way of what he wanted most to do. As one of the reactions against whatever frustrated his felicity this poem is an impeccable performance.

4

Scrutiny of the poems devoted to Church and religion leaves us puzzled, rather than better informed, about the development of Rimbaud's religious feelings. His youthful devotion to republicanism naturally implies a strong anticlerical bias. As an institution, the Church had been a bastion of the Second Empire, and had looked an even stronger one than it was. Furthermore, the boy had been in contact, through his teachers, with a laicism which, though not yet so strong as when it dominated the national school system after the war, posited a state of constant competition between Church and lay schools for the right to educate the young. Neither his political allegiance, nor his feeling for teachers like Izambard, would have been anything for Rimbaud to take lightly. And in addition, the Church was all entangled in his relationship with his mother, standing for the respectability she prized, and sanctioning—in her mind, at least—the prohibitions she enforced. It stood beside her, between him and happiness.

A curious image presides over Rimbaud's expressed feelings on this subject: God is either absent or uninterested or else sunk in a deep sleep which only the clink of money can interrupt. Being in a church is less the experience of being in the house of God than of being in the home of a permanent stench. The walls, washed every hundred years, stink; the people stink; the curé's shoes have fermented. The poor come in a state of misery which stirs him to little compassion, and the rich bring an ill-health which makes them repulsive. The mothers of the war dead, the destitute, and the children come to pray, or to sit without praying, amid the bad smells distilled from all the similar generations which have gone before. And meanwhile the flashing altar is as separate as if in another world—the Real Absence. God is elsewhere.

Yet only one of the three poems that bear directly upon religion reaches the aggressive bitterness with which he lashes out at other restrictive forces in his life. Whereas "Les Pauvres à l'église" is principally occupied with an additional instance of an ugliness which he finds everywhere in Charleville, "Les Premières Communions," with its frequently quoted description of juvenile religious hysteria, seems truly intent upon heaping abomination on abomination, blasphemy on blasphemy. Rimbaud's sister was making her first communion during this year, and the thought of it must have irritated him greatly. One may also suspect that the account of a girl's slipping from a nervousness natural in such situations into a fever of morbid sexuality is based upon factual observation.

But, at the same time, the poem is devoted to an extremely familiar *topos*. We may find originality as well as blasphemy in lines like these:

> Et mon cœur et ma chair par ta chair embrassée
> Fourmillent du baiser putride de Jésus!

Yet, in spite of the image of death and corruption, this is only a variation on the neopagan theme that Christianity is a sickness which has supplanted the healthiness of a sunny, pagan Golden Age, such as is most familiar to English and American readers from Swinburne's "Garden of Proserpine";

> Thou hast conquered, O pale Galilean!
> The world has grown gray from thy breath:
> We have drunken of things Lethean,
> And fed on the fulness of death.

The idea had been commonplace in France since the first hellenizing of the generation of 1840.

Without directly challenging the conviction, held by many, that Rimbaud's inspiration in this poem is deeply personal, one may point out that it combines elements of "Soleil et chair" with others of "Vénus anadyomène": in addition to being an attack upon Christianity, through the Eucharist, it is also one upon the modern world for falling short of an ideal. It is impossible not to take this poem, along with the other poems of the same year on this subject, to be a rejection of the Church, but perhaps less of the Church in general than of the specific examples of it with which, as an unwilling citizen of Charleville, Rimbaud had to live. The residual impression they leave is one of something unpleasant, unclean, and ugly. But this is also the impression left by what he had to say about other things in the old home town, and one is reminded that Charleville fell short of more than one ideal.

5

He was not, for example, pleased by the treatment he got from the librarians who grumbled at going to find the books he asked for. According to his biographers he had little to do but read or take walks, and if indeed he read even a fraction of the total which various critics credit him with — since otherwise he would not have known what they think he knew —

he cannot have spent much time walking. His slight figure may well have become irritatingly familiar to elderly functionaries who disliked being disturbed. Once more he relieves his aggressive tendencies, and this time in a poem noteworthy for its savage eloquence, "Les Assis":

Noirs de loupes, grêlés, les yeux cerclés de bagues
Vertes, leurs doigts boulus crispés à leurs fémurs,
Le sinciput plaqué de hargnosités vagues
Comme les floraisons lépreuses des vieux murs;

Ils ont greffé dans des amours épileptiques
Leur fantasque ossature aux grands squelettes noirs
De leurs chaises; leurs pieds aux barreaux rachitiques
S'entrelacent pour les matins et pour les soirs!

Ces vieillards ont toujours fait tresse avec leurs sièges,
Sentant les soleils vifs percaliser leur peau,
Ou, les yeux à la vitre où se fanent les neiges,
Tremblant du tremblement douloureux du crapaud.

Et les Sièges leur ont des bontés: culottée
De brun, la paille cède aux angles de leurs reins;
L'âme des vieux soleils s'allume emmaillotée
Dans ces tresses d'épis où fermentaient les grains.

. . . .

– Oh! ne les faites pas lever! C'est le naufrage . . .
Ils surgissent, grondant comme des chats giflés,
Ouvrant lentement leurs omoplates, ô rage!
Tout leur pantalon bouffe à leurs reins boursouflés.

Et vous les écoutez, cognant leurs têtes chauves
Aux murs sombres, plaquant et plaquant leurs pieds tors,
Et leurs boutons d'habit sont des prunelles fauves
Qui vous accrochent l'œil du fond des corridors!

The picture is not without humor, but the total effect can hardly be called humorous. These old men, librarians or not, are meant first and foremost to be unpleasant to look at. Figures involving the leprous, rachitic, epileptic, skeletal, and venomous, along with evocations of dogs, cats, and toads, and images of bodies grown into the structure of chairs and of chairs encrusted in dirt leave nothing on which the eye may rest in comfort. Rimbaud mercilessly catalogues everything repulsive about the wrinkled, discolored, sagging skin, the bald and trembling heads, the contorted bodies, twisted feet, and flapping wattles. As in "Vénus anadyomène" his eye moves methodically from detail to detail, missing none: "Tout leur pantalon bouffe à leurs reins boursouflés." There is no lesson for him to draw; the description is enough. If you disturb one of these he will go grumping off with the buttons on his coat shining like the eyes of wild animals, and return looking at you so poisonously that you break out in sweat. At the end, inevitably, comes the scabrous detail: "Et leur membre s'agace à des barbes d'épis." What one has already suspected on reading "Vénus anadyomène," that Rimbaud had learned early how to convey distaste through the tone of a description, here becomes only too obvious.

The same pitiless eye is at work in "Accroupissements," and the subject itself—a man crouched upon a chamber-pot—assures the presence of an adequate amount of obscenity. But one learns from the poem little about Rimbaud that one did not know before. It is further evidence that he was in a mood to befoul, a mood which extends into several other poems. The unhappy children of "Les Poètes de sept ans," and the girl in "Les Premières Communions," squat for hours in latrines; and in "Oraison du soir" the poet pictures himself in a café garden, urinating violently. Later, when he has got away to Paris, there will be numerous stories about his abominable conduct. One may hope that the tale about his having defecated in Banville's breakfast milk is apocryphal, but poems like "Accroupissements" lend a certain psychological credibility: he was evidently capable of imagining some rather horrid things. This great poet was, among other things, a very repulsive little boy upon occasion, and possibly a sick one. There are moments during the winter of 1870–1871 when it would seem that he is not satisfied with befouling what he touches in order to take revenge for his discomfort. Some of his aggressiveness can be understood as aimed at himself.

6

In his sweeping rejections he includes love, and here it is hard to see how Charleville could be at fault. He reveals now the first glimpse of a mechanism which he will use more openly later, after the discoveries recorded in the "Lettre du voyant," and whose working will underlie the entire *Saison en enfer*. This is the rejection of some previously important part of his attitude toward the world—which he now feels to be delusive.

"Mes petites amoureuses" turns in violent and obscene anger upon the population of his nympholeptic day dreams. "Que d'amours j'ai rêvées," he had exclaimed in one of the happy moments of fugue. Now the phrase is replaced by: "Que je vous hais." The loved ones he had once dreamed of he now simply hates. Attempts to discover in this poem a first expression of Rimbaud's latent homosexuality, based on the assumption that he is saying farewell to young women he had actually known, are probably excessive. What evidence is there that he had ever known, not to say known carnally, any young women at all?

More to the point is his violence:

> Nous nous aimions à cette époque,
> Bleu laideron!

On mangeait des œufs à la coque
Et du mouron!

Un soir, tu me sacras poète,
Blond laideron:
Descends ici, que je te fouette
En mon giron;

J'ai dégueulé ta bandoline,
Noir laideron;
Tu couperais ma mandoline
Au fil du front.

Pouah! mes salives desséchées,
Roux laideron,
Infectent encor les tranchées
De ton sein rond!

O mes petites amoureuses,
Que je vous hais!
Plaquez de fouffes douloureuses
Vos tétons laids!

These female horrors of the poem—a "laideron" has to be frightfully ugly—blue (*sic*), blond, black, and red-headed, seem most likely to be only the partners of early erotic phantasies like "Première soirée." But the word "only," in this context, devaluates something which before this had real value: the phantasies were a normal part of the happiness he celebrated so often, and, the poem remarks, a source of his poetry:

Et c'est pourtant pour ces éclanches
Que j'ai rimé!
Je voudrais vous casser les hanches
D'avoir aimé!

Although places in these stanzas seem overtly sadistic, one may be reasonably sure that the total mood is intrapunitive. This poem should be read with its companion, "Les Sœurs de charité," which expresses at once disappointment in love and what Freudians could not fail to recognize as the death wish. In a Baudelairian mood this time, he again rejects women, but now not in anger; woman cannot cure the "eternal and deep wound," and consequently cannot be the source of the final, effective consolation the Young Man in the poem seeks. His "sœur de charité," then, can be only death.

This was what it was like to spend a winter in Charleville when he wanted to be elsewhere. The war was awful; the men who made it were hateful or ridiculous; the townspeople were stuffy and stupid, or else, as in "L'Homme juste," detestable. Churches were ugly and smelly; his mother was an ogress; and, worst of all, the old sources of felicity had failed. And so his tone varies from pity for the victims of this life to indignation, irony, and invective. There is at least some satisfaction for him, though perverse, in giving offense and even in desecration.

What was the way out? Apparently fugue remained in his mind as the characteristic access to happiness. Yet the literal, physical possibility of departing on foot across country, preferably toward Paris, was doomed in advance. Fortunately, another kind of fugue was available, the flight of the imagination. He seized upon it. Sometime late in the winter of his discontent he discovered the inherent promise of his ingrained tendency toward phantasy—perhaps not long before the day, on or about May 15, 1871, when he wrote his friend Demeny the now famous "Lettre du voyant." Its subject is exactly this fugue of the imagination and how it may be contrived.

Shortly thereafter he would contrive one, and it would be called "Le Bateau ivre."

Chapter IV — Hallucination and Epiphany

BECAUSE RIMBAUD had tumbled upon a theory of poetic practice which was new to him, he assumed that it was new to the world at large. New, as it happens, is the thing it was most precisely not. There are so many possible sources for his ideas that delighted scholars lose themselves completely in the welter. It is now commonplace that the "Lettre du voyant" is a radical departure — and that for two generations French poetry had already been intent on going in the direction it points! * Many of its ideas are, in any case, far more than two generations old. Perhaps, if Rimbaud had given his old teacher the opportunity, Izambard would have told him so. But Izambard did not have the opportunity: the letter went to Charles Demeny.

Why Izambard was not the recipient is clear enough. He

* A translation of the "Lettre du voyant" begins on page 233.

had just gone back to his place in the public school system instead of accepting one offered him in Russia, an act which struck Rimbaud as little less than crawling back to make a private peace with the regime. In his letter of May 13, in which he makes reference to his new theory but does not develop it, he also makes clear his opinion that Izambard has returned to the trough, adding that henceforth he expects little of Izambard's own poetry. The suggestion that Rimbaud hesitated to tell his teacher more because he wanted sympathetic understanding and was not sure of getting it is an understatement. The "Lettre du voyant" was to be ornamented by the inclusion of poems in which the adolescent's revolt was expressed with a vigor which would likely have indisposed Izambard at his most indulgent. Even if Rimbaud had not chosen to tell him that the return to teaching was an example of taking a coward's way, and joined with this the arrogant assurance that now Izambard's poetry would come to naught, Izambard could hardly have seemed a receptive audience. It was better strategy to tell him just enough to whet his curiosity and send him some enigmatic poems, reserving the details of the good news for Demeny. Actually it makes no difference whether Rimbaud's ideas were new or not, so long as he put them into practice. But the cold water he might have got from Izambard could conceivably have changed the history of a hundred years of French poetry.

2

Everything points to his wanting a well-disposed audience, even though, as usual, the fact is not entirely beyond challenge: at this, as at so many other turning points in Rimbaud's life, the chronology is blurred. The date of the letter to Izambard, May 13, is certain; but the one assigned the letter to Demeny by Mouquet, in the Pléiade edition, is conjectural—and the conjecture seems based on nothing more than the feeling that, since the letter to Demeny deals in detail with matter which is only adumbrated in the one to Izambard, the fuller letter must be the later written. Nothing really proves that when Rimbaud wrote Izambard his theories were not just as fully formed as when he wrote to Demeny, and the impression Mouquet's edition causes, of a vertiginous development of the ideas, by putting the Demeny letter second and dating it, between brackets, two days later, has little support in objective fact. Surely nothing justifies concluding that Demeny got the "Lettre du voyant" just because Rimbaud, having written Izambard before his ideas had fully jelled, did not want to write him again so soon. And to top these considerations, the letter itself testifies to his desire for a sympathetic hearing.

"J'ai résolu de vous donner une heure de littérature nouvelle. Je commence de suite par un psaume d'actualité." The very first line, offering his correspondent an "hour of new literature," is a bid for special attention. And the second, announcing the "psaume d'actualité" to follow immediately, establishes the curious pattern of alternate inflation and deflation, rise and fall, which is characteristic of the entire letter: first the portentous statement, then the self-deprecating retirement to a lower key. Repeatedly the excited declaration is followed by the quieter side remark, as if to warn the reader not to take too seriously what the writer himself takes with a grain of salt. From his next subsequent letter to Demeny, June 10, we know beyond doubt that by then Rimbaud had come to take his ideas very seriously indeed; probably he did so from the start. But the "Lettre du voyant" does not prove his seriousness; it leaves his reader guessing about how much the poet really means of what he says.

— Voici de la prose sur l'avenir de la poésie: —

Toute poésie antique aboutit à la poésie grecque, Vie harmonieuse.— De la Grèce au mouvement romantique, — moyen-âge, — il y a des lettrés, des versificateurs. D'Ennius à Theroldus, de Theroldus à Casimir Delavigne, tout est prose rimée, un jeu, avachissement et gloire d'innombrables générations idiotes: Racine est le pur, le fort, le grand. — On eût soufflé sur ses rimes, brouillé ses hémistiches, que le Divin Sot serait aujourd'hui aussi ignoré que le premier venu auteur d'*Origines*. — Après Racine, le jeu moisit. Il a duré deux mille ans!

The "psalm" having turned out to be Rimbaud's "Chant de guerre parisien," Rimbaud returns to his note of facetiousness in the announcement that next will come "a prose on the future of poetry." Again the pitch rises as he sweeps away most of the history of European literature, from the Greeks right down to French Romanticism. The statements are categorical and violent. He sees nothing good in the centuries between the Greeks and Racine, and after Racine the game goes stale again. And with the break of the paragraph the pitch drops. "Ni plaisanterie, ni paradoxe. La raison m'inspire plus de certitudes sur le sujet que n'aurait jamais eu de colères un Jeune-France. Du reste, libre aux *nouveaux* d'exécrer les ancêtres: on est chez soi et l'on a le temps."

Telling one's reader not to look for jokes or paradoxes is probably the best way discovered to date of showing one's awareness of sounding overserious; Demeny is alerted to the possibility that there is some kind of exaggeration here. The next sentence, about being fuller of certainty than the notoriously irascible Jeunes-France poets had been of wrath, is indeed a joke. The remark about how newcomers are free to execrate their precursors is mild self-disparagement. The return to solid earth is complete.

But immediately he sets out on a longer, higher flight:

On n'a jamais bien jugé le romantisme. Qui l'aurait jugé? les

Critiques!! Les Romantiques? qui prouvent si bien que la chanson est si peu souvent l'œuvre, c'est-à-dire la pensée chantée et comprise du chanteur?

Car Je est un autre. Si le cuivre s'éveille clairon, il n'y a rien de sa faute. Cela m'est évident: j'assiste à l'éclosion de ma pensée: je la regarde, je l'écoute: je lance un coup d'archet: la symphonie fait son remuement dans les profondeurs, ou vient d'un bond sur la scène.

He has turned serious again. From his criticism of the Romantics—what they achieved was a happy accident and entirely unplanned; they, themselves, did not understand it—on through the famous declaration that the Ego is someone else there is no let-down, but a tension which, perhaps, even increases as he continues. And he sustains this pitch, through his exposition of the consequences of his discovery and of the discipline which the poet must impose upon himself, as far as the climax which foresees the possibilities of great reward—or of ultimate individual failure.

Je dis qu'il faut être *voyant,* se faire *voyant.*

Le Poète se fait *voyant* par un long, immense et raisonné *dérèglement* de *tous les sens.* Toutes les formes d'amour, de souffrance, de folie; il cherche lui-même, il épuise en lui tous les poisons, pour n'en garder que les quintessences. Ineffable torture où il a besoin de toute la foi, de toute la force surhumaine, où il devient entre tous le grand malade, le grand criminel, le grand maudit,—et le suprême Savant!—Car il arrive à l'*inconnu!* Puisqu'il a cultivé son âme, déjà riche, plus qu'aucun! Il arrive à l'inconnu, et quand, affolé, il finirait par perdre l'intelligence de ses visions, il les a vues! Qu'il crève dans son bondissement par les choses inouïes et innommables: viendront d'autres horribles travailleurs; ils commenceront par les horizons où l'autre s'est affaissé!

And now, when it is impossible to strain higher, sound and sense having risen together to the portals of the unknown and then come tumbling down, the poet's tone comes tumbling after. "To be continued," says the single sentence of the next paragraph, "in six minutes."

Here for a moment we may put aside what a century, roughly, has taught us about the importance of this letter in the history of literature and remember only that its author was a sensitive, self-conscious youth who a few months before this had behaved as if the whole activity of literature were a performance. He is still a performer here—one who, having reached the peak of his passion, has suddenly stopped, acknowledged the presence of his audience with an invitation to remain for the next act, and walked off the stage. There could be no better way of showing not only that this *is* a performance but also that the performer recognizes himself for what he is. This is why the letter had to go to Demeny rather than to Izambard.

The question of sincerity does not arise. There is not the least sign of Rimbaud's not meaning exactly what he says. But it is true that he is leaving himself a loophole: if his reader refuses to take him seriously a retreat is always open; he can save a sensitive face by pretending that he has not been taking himself seriously, either.

He is also being a performer in another sense: he is not merely declaring that "Je" is someone else but also demonstrating it. He has been doing, right here in this letter, what he says the Romantics failed to do: dividing his psyche so that one half has departed in a visionary flight while the other has guided the process, remained fully conscious, and exercised direction.

And knowing now what Rimbaud is up to we may return to inspect the performance, or what we have seen of it so far, and to admire other aspects of it which have been obscured by our concern for the rise and fall of tension. For, for the first time in his life so far as we know, he is writing the kind of prose he will use in *Une Saison en enfer*. He may not yet be the man of this later work, but already his vocabulary, syntax, and imagery suggest those of his full maturity.

Undeniably, Rimbaud's vocabulary here has a flavor of bombast about it which the later writings happily lack. The insistent repetition in the last paragraph of *tous* and *toutes,* the prevalence of words like *maudit, criminel, crève, bondissement, inouïes, innommables, horribles travailleurs,* the repetition of *grand,* strike one as less obedient to the emotions involved than as responding to the need to impress a reader with the size of the enterprise. But the violent tone itself seems authentic, and we recognize instantly the effort to achieve absolute and incontrovertible statement which dictates choice. It is as if Rimbaud felt that if he made his statements strong enough they could never be confuted. And it is probably the force of this vocabulary which leaves the feeling that something has been left suspended in space whenever Rimbaud relaxes the tension of his discourse.

The mounting tension and excitement of this section of the letter are conveyed no more by the words themselves, however, than by the special sentence structure. Rimbaud's vehicle, here as later, is the simple assertion, the straight declarative sentence. Relative clauses are rare—he is not interested in qualifying. The prevailing mood is intensely indicative; he is not leaving room for implied doubt. The declarations, in the moments of intensity, are short and staccato: "Cela m'est évident: j'assiste à l'éclosion de ma pensée: je la regarde, je l'écoute." Such prose is as rapid as the narrative prose of Diderot, which in French sets the standard, imitating the contours of excited speech. Even the punctuation is revealing. The first colon is the only one to play the colon's usual role of introducing an explanation; the others in the passage merely prevent the rushing statements from blurring with each other

—or even from stumbling over each other, as they seem constantly threatening to do. Half of the punctuation in the letter as a whole is used only to exercise this control. The absence of conjunctions is noteworthy: juxtaposition alone does the work of logical ordering, and at times the thought is correspondingly hard to follow. Example: "Des fonctionnaires, des écrivains: auteur, créateur, poète, cet homme n'a jamais existé," by which he means, "there have been bureaucrats and scribblers, but the true author, creator, poet—such a man has not yet existed." The amount of interpreting the reader must do if he is to catch the full sense indicates the breadth of the ellipses across which the mind must leap.

As the development approaches its climax declaration tends to give way to ejaculation. The exclamation point becomes characteristic. And we begin to hear the prophetic voice which disdains proof because whatever it says is true by virtue of being enunciated. Twice the sentences take the form which will become habitual in the *Illuminations* and *Une Saison en enfer*: the subject is set down first as a kind of absolute, unrelated to a principal verb: "Toutes les formes d'amour, de souffrance, de folie"; "ineffable torture." What would normally form the remainder of the sentence follows by itself, as a separate sentence, as if it were the elaboration of a previously stated theme.

Hence, it must be added, this prose has the prophet's incoherence as well as the prophet's tone. It is no wonder, really, that the "Lettre du voyant" is so easy to misread. The text is incoherent in the same way as the later prose poems: these truths are so completely self-evident to Rimbaud's mind, so clear already, that he will not be bothered making them fully and precisely communicative. The technique is suggestive of that of certain primitives who assume that the act of naming a thing is all that is needed to bring it into being.

The images which leap out of the pages are also typical: the brute material which, unaware, metamorphoses into an instrument; the musician who is at once conductor and orchestra; the man grafting warts on his own face; the poet becoming Prometheus by virtue of his suffering; the poet, again, falling back broken by the violence of his experience. They testify to the incomplete rationality of what Rimbaud is trying to say: he is feeling his notion of the poet-seer rather than thinking it, and the images are more a part of the statement that the passage as a whole is designed to make than an illustration of the central idea with which they purport to be associated. We are forced to conclude that the text, again taken as a whole, aims to exhibit something rather than to communicate it discursively. And this, in turn, seems not unconnected with images that identify the poet as performer.

Indeed, we must not forget that the performance which he is creating in the letter itself—as distinguished from the one pictured in the imagery—is a calculated effect. For it is now, after he has whipped himself into the excited incoherence of the image of the poet mounting in a great leap toward the Unknown, that he suddenly suspends the show. The conductor's baton stops still at the top of a beat. "To be continued in six minutes." The gesture contributes generously to the total of what the letter has to say.

The momentary effect upon the reader, as we were saying, is to return him to solid ground. And there Rimbaud intends to keep him for a while. The performer returns to the podium with the baton firmly in hand; and intent on giving a controlled performance. We are as far as possible from the manic mood which preceded the intermission, and remain completely relaxed through the interval occasioned by his introducing the poem "Mes petites amoureuses" in the text. When this is done he inserts a parenthesis explaining that other poems could be included also, to a total length of over three hundred lines of verse, except for his not having money to pay postage. This is one of the two places in the entire text where his style concedes, even momentarily, that this performance is in the form of a letter.

The total length of the intermission and the space of low tension which follows it may escape the reader for reasons having to do with typography: the texts of the poems Rimbaud included in the letter are represented in the available editions only by the titles followed by one line of suspension points. To appreciate the performance qua performance it is necessary each time to read into the appropriate space the poem indicated, which in the present instance means reading twelve quatrains before the equilibrium of high and low tension passages can be felt and the principle establish itself that the higher the previous excitement, the longer the following low interval will be.

But never again does the tension quite reach the point attained just before this break. Rimbaud goes on to the consequences of his discovery for poetry, the form that the poet's vision of the Unknown may take or its possible lack of form, the new language which will have to be developed, the necessity of a return to something like the poetry of the Greeks, and the emergence of the New Woman as poet. Then, after a transitional paragraph which admits that all this cannot come at once and that meanwhile the poet may properly be expected only to furnish something "New," the letter moves into a discussion of nineteenth-century poetry in France and the extent to which various individual poets succeeded in being *voyant*. To judge by the relative incoherence of the sentence structure and the prevalence of exclamation points, the first half of this part aspires to greater intensity than the second, but the upsurge is not entirely continuous and lacks force; the second half subsides until finally it ends with a catalogue of names. Irony (about such targets as Musset, and the "génie" which inhabited Rabelais, Voltaire, and La Fontaine, and furnished a subject for Hippolyte Taine) replaces direct statement and is obviously too self-conscious to permit reaching any real height.

The letter finishes with another example of self-deprecation, in which Rimbaud refers to the poem he now copies into the text as another "chant pieux"—that is, another "psalm"—which turns out to be "Accroupissements," and a valedictory urging Demeny to reply soon.

3

An account of the habitual repetitions of Rimbaud's imagination must not overlook the similarity in emotional pattern between this letter and what we gather from the poems to have been the shape of his actual fugues. Admittedly our information about the fugues is scanty: no friend accompanied him to whom we may turn for reminiscences, and Rimbaud left no record other than the poems. Even so, they cannot but have begun in excitement and exaltation, rising to the moments of beatitude which are the subjects of the fugue poems; and they cannot have ended in other than a much lower emotional key. We have seen the letter rising to a peak of tension—rising always, despite the alternations of inflation and deflation which have been noted—at the point where Rimbaud reveals the hope of knowing the Unknown. Here, to point the contrast, is the final full paragraph:

> Rompue aux formes vieilles—parmi les innocents, A. Renaud,—a fait son Rolla; L. Grandet,—a fait son Rolla;—les gaulois et les Mussets, G. Lafenestre, Coran, Cl. Popelin, Soulary, L. Salles; les écoliers, Marc. Aicard, Theuriet; les morts et les imbéciles, Autran, Barbier, L. Pichat, Lemoyne, les Deschamps, les Des Essarts; les journalistes, L. Cladel, Robert Luzarches, X. de Ricard; les fan-

taisistes, C. Mendès; les bohèmes; les femmes; les talents, Léon Dierx et Sully-Prudhomme, Coppée, — la nouvelle école, dite parnassienne, a deux voyants, Albert Mérat et Paul Verlaine, un vrai poète. — Voilà. — Ainsi je travaille à me rendre *voyant*. — Et finissons par un chant pieux.

In this listing of successful and unsuccessful poets the letter may hardly be said to reach a conclusion. It merely trails off.

Between form of letter and form of fugue there is similarity enough to invite speculation, and the speculation is an interesting one, especially since the pattern of tensions in the letter is repeated in a number of poems which he will write in the succeeding year and a half: relatively early in each he reaches the climactic peak of emotional intensity, after which the tension and excitement can only decline. In some, as a matter of fact, the gradual loss of tension will be the subject of the poem itself; much of Rimbaud's poetry is more "self-reflexive" than it is usually credited with being. All of these, in whatever degree they make the experience of writing a poem their subject, appear in the Rimbaud canon after the date of the "Lettre du voyant." It would thus seem that with the letter a new aspect of habitual imaginative behavior comes into view. The consequences should become apparent upon closer inspection of the poems involved.

Another conclusion to be drawn from considering the letter as a performance is that greater emphasis must inevitably be placed upon the ideas that are introduced in the passages where tension grades most sharply upward. They are: the discovery of the double, or split, personality, one half of which performs while the other directs and controls and which will henceforth allow the poet to do intentionally what his predecessors have done only by accident; the discovery that this division may be cultivated through the use of various forms of stimulation, so that it may be made to occur at the will of the poet; and the notion of a special kind of vision or knowledge or intelligence which the poet may obtain. These now assume an importance, in comparison to the ideas in the rest of the letter, which is hardly apparent so long as the letter is analyzed only according to its logical structure. Accordingly, various critics have been hardly more concerned with them than with such problems as what Rimbaud meant by his reference to the need for a "new" language or to the eventual emergence of woman as poet. Their attention has been monopolized by the logical structure, and in truth much of their effort has gone into shoring up the structure itself. It needs so much shoring, actually, that the effort hardly pays for itself, and may even result in falsification, especially if the answer to what Rimbaud may have meant by his cryptic remarks in the later paragraphs is that he did not really know himself. Even if he knew perfectly what he meant the fact would make very little difference, and where he got the ideas, in the works of Eliphas Lévy or elsewhere, even less.

It should be clear, after more than sixty years of exegesis, that none of the materials of the "Lettre du voyant" are particularly new. What he may have meant by his "JE est un autre" has been the subject of endless speculation. The phrase cannot but excite the amateur psychologist. But we are not necessarily contemplating a case of incipient schizophrenia. Any number of imaginative men have discovered two principles in their egos, one active and one passive: most of us are aware of a dissociation within ourselves of the part which presides over snaffle and bit and the part which is bloody 'orse. The conviction that the creative personality is so organized is ancient. Nothing in the "Lettre du voyant" authorizes the belief that Rimbaud had discovered at this point anything which Pascal (for example), no few Romantic poets, and even the Musset he detested so much did not know. If he thought he had, the truth still stands that it takes more than genius to make a lad of seventeen realize to what extent his experience merely recapitulates that of the race. It is certain that he feels that to have such a divisible ego is in itself a destiny. So much the worse, he says both to Demeny and to Izambard, for the man who feels himself to be so constructed, as for the wood which discovers that it has become a violin or for the metal suddenly turned into a trumpet.

What excites him is much less the psychological discovery than his perception of what can be made of it. His variation on what is after all a rather common theme is his notion that the passive, observing part of the psyche, instead of exercising a merely negative disciplinary function, can be set to directing the other in excursions increasingly further afield. His complaint about the Romantics, that they had the capacity to be *voyants* but used it only by chance—even Baudelaire, he says, entertained a concept of art which trammeled him very seriously indeed—makes it manifest that he does not think of himself as the exclusive possessor of a unique gift. His emphasis is on knowing how to use it.

Such emphases should be carefully preserved. The habit of his interpreters, in reading the celebrated sentence about his method ("Le poète se fait *voyant* par un long, immense, et raisonné *dérèglement* de *tous les sens*") has been to give deep attention to the words in italic—as of course they should—but to scant those left in roman, especially the word "raisonné." The senses will not only be thrown out of normal gear, but the process will be methodical and planned. What Baudelaire and Rimbaud's other predecessors had not had, most clearly, was method. They had failed to realize that the poet can train himself to perceive the Unknown.

Just what the Unknown is Rimbaud does not say, for the reason, unexceptionable in the circumstances, that at the moment of writing Demeny his discovery of it necessarily lies in the future. Some writers have taken it to be a synonym for God, and have been encouraged to do so by Rimbaud's remark, made when he was disgusted with himself and disappointed in his poetic enterprise, that he had confused himself with the Almighty. Even if we take this outburst at its face value, it may very well mean no more than that he had been foolish enough to aspire to knowledge which alone the Deity could possess. There is a good chance that in 1871 he meant even less. The tradition of the poet's being a seer who possesses special knowledge goes back at least as far as the Gaelic bards; and Baudelaire had made of the *Inconnu* a region somewhere out of this world where one might escape ennui through meeting entirely new experience. Rimbaud may only have been pushing Baudelaire's doctrine of a special understanding of the universe based upon the perception of metaphor — the universe being but a vast reservoir of metaphors — one step further.

In actual practice, what he seems to have had in mind was the ability to induce hallucination at will. Such at least would appear to be the end product of an ordered and calculated disordering of the senses. Rimbaud does not use the word "hallucination" in the letter. Only when he comes, in *Une Saison en enfer,* to have doubts about his method, will he spell it out — and then in disparagement. But how could he have meant anything else?

In a sense he was only carrying Baudelaire's idea to its limit. Hallucination is, after all, the ultimate step in the formation of metaphor. Since Diderot at the latest, we have known that its components are not new to the hallucinated individual: the visionary who sees a dog using lobster claws for legs would be right in taking the monster to be unknown, but there is nothing new about either dogs or lobsters. What is new is the experience of a relationship: the hallucination has dislocated two perfectly familiar elements of our ordinary world and put them into a thoroughly unfamiliar, because unique, reassociation. Had the visionary called the dog's legs lobster claws while remaining aware that they *were* legs, he would have been playing the double game of metaphor. In other words, hallucination is metaphor masquerading as literal experience.

Just how hallucination is supposed to lead to the Unknown, except in the mechanical sense adumbrated above, he does not say. The poet, we learn, becomes Prometheus. This is all.

And not enough, even though we may learn something from the particular image of Prometheus he proposes. This is Prometheus the stealer of fire, beyond doubt, but not particularly the defiant Prometheus, the father of cosmic revolt; instead, this is the Prometheus of the damaged liver, condemned for his exploit and accursed—even though the possessor of a knowledge which is of transcendent value to Man. One might be justified in feeling that what the image reflects, more than anything else, is a foreboding of defeat.

Various other references, such as the one to the poet's being "awakened" or the one to his participating in the "great dream," suggest the language of the nineteenth-century adepts of the esoteric. So also, perhaps, does his remark about the Universal Intelligence which has always cast off its ideas "naturally" (that is, presumably, without being forced by the adventurous poet to do so). But on the whole one has the feeling of groping about in a forest of half-formed ideas.

Possibly this is all he tells us because it is all, at the writing, that he has to say. There is at least one indication in the letter that Rimbaud had not thought the matter through. At the end, he lists among poets who have reached some degree of voyancy Leconte de Lisle, Théodore de Banville, and Théophile Gautier. Gautier has enjoyed special esteem in America because he was taken as a model by Ezra Pound and the Imagists, but it is doubtful whether his work is much read, here or elsewhere—even though it did not fully deserve, perhaps, André Gide's dismissal as "jovial banality." And whatever the claims of Leconte de Lisle and Banville to immortality, they are certainly thought of as skillful, knowledgeable craftsmen more often than as seers. Rimbaud's including the now completely forgotten Albert Mérat is even more surprising. Yet he puts these names among the "très voyants."

We know from his parodies that Rimbaud was a more than adequate literary critic. There is ample evidence in his work that he was quite familiar with the poems of Gautier, Leconte de Lisle, and Banville—if not of Mérat. The only way out of this dilemma is to admit that he had not fully decided what he was talking about.

4

All in all, the letter tells us less about voyancy, and about Rimbaud, than we would like. His excited talk about visions makes one wonder whether he had not discovered himself to be what June E. Downey, in *The Creative Imagination,* calls an *Eidetiker.*

The "eidetic" image is characterized by extreme vividness, and richness in detail, and by seeming to possess the independent existence of a conceptual object. Such an image, says Miss Downey, is one in which "a former perception is actually seen, not merely imagined." Summing up much previous research, she adds that while eidetic imagery is a common phenomenon of childhood, there are relatively few adults capable of it: the capacity diminishes or disappears after adolescence. She quotes Jaensch, the one time leader of the "Marburg School," to the effect that there are even two types of eidetic image, one of a flexible and variable sort, common among artists, which occurs spontaneously and is pleasant to experience, and another which masters its possessor and is so obsessive as to make him uncomfortable. In either case, it seems, the images can be "of almost hallucinatory vividness."

But was Rimbaud an *Eidetiker*? Miss Downey does not identify him as such, but she does mention a number of other poets who were not entirely unlike him. William Blake was apparently so successful in invoking brilliant images that he could even teach his wife "to pray them up." Coleridge, interrupted in the midst of his opium dream of Kublai Khan by the man from Porlock, would seem to have had less complete control of the same instrument, but would also seem to be very like Rimbaud in using artificial stimulants to loosen his ties with reality and allow his brilliant images to dissociate and then re-form in new associations more or less beyond his control. Rimbaud would be still young enough for the eidetic images to have retained their brilliance, and at the same time old enough to have discovered his poetic process; the new associations would seem to exist objectively and could easily seem more real than the phenomena of his ordinary world.

The "Lettre du voyant" is far from telling us what we would like to know, also, about the *process* of attaining the hallucinated trance or when he began putting it into practice. Rimbaud says that the poet must render his soul "monstrous," of course, like the man who grafts warts on the skin of his own face, and that he must contrive to be superlatively sick, criminal, and accursed. His letter to Izambard speaks of his purposefully becoming a good-for-nothing ("Je m'encrapule") and a sponger of drinks. Nothing could be harder to verify, but some have believed that he was experimenting, tentatively, with women—although when he speaks of his consumption of "bocks" and "filles" there is an excellent chance that he meant *filles* in the local Ardennais sense of wine bottles. A bit later, having left home, he would be free to try such other expedients as the abuse of tobacco, coffee, tea, and insomnia. It has also been assumed that exhaustion following protracted masturbation was another, immediately available, means of attaining a hallucinated state.

For narcotics he probably had to wait until he got to Paris, where, we know, he tried smoking hashish. But he speaks of his "enormous sufferings" in the present tense, as if he were already embarked on his experiment with hallucinants while still in Charleville.

We are forced to notice, also, that when Rimbaud talks about the ways and means of his enterprise he is never far from falling into hyperbole. "All the forms of love, of suffering, of folly . . . he (the poet) exhausts all the poisons and keeps only the quintessences. Unspeakable torture." This is the language of melodrama.

Was the suffering really so great? The persistent abuse of the superlative makes one the least bit doubtful. Can it be that he was in fact experiencing some discomfort but exaggerating its intensity? Or even, that he was in no discomfort at all, but felt, for the dignity of his newly discovered poetic process, that he *should* be so? We cannot say, but there is no denying a real discrepancy between the grandiose ends the young poet wants to attain, and the cheap banality of the means at his disposal. There is some reason to suspect the presence of more ritualism than reality in his recipe.

Rimbaud's process conforms only too closely to a familiar formula. An individual of unusual intensity and sensitivity feels himself chosen for a special fate, and perhaps estranged from his fellows at the same time; he feels forced, more or less against his will, to withdraw into either exile or seclusion; during his separation and absence he undergoes a painful ordeal — of a nature which he is rarely able to explain — but emerges from it in possession of new and precious knowledge; he will henceforth be a specially endowed creature, of exceptional value both in his own eyes and in those of his tribe.

Roughly, this is the ritual pattern of the shaman's initiation —withdrawal, ordeal, enlightenment, return. Rimbaud's program is so like it that we cannot but ponder how suspiciously appropriate it is that the prophet should suffer in the wilderness before being vouchsafed the message he subsequently brings the world. And, remembering that he is putting on a performance for Demeny's benefit (as well as his own), we doubtless do well not to take the matter of suffering too literally. His discomfort impresses us much less than the use he intends to make of it.

5

The importance of his ordeal, whether real or ritualistic, lies in his regarding it not as a subject of poetry but as an instrument. It is not to be something to write about, but an initiation qualifying him to write about something else. This specifies a definitive rupture with French Romanticism and perhaps with Romanticism everywhere: the gambit of the Pageant of the Bleeding Heart, which has been the controlling one in poetry from Lamartine to Baudelaire, is here abandoned at long last. Hugo and Musset had sung their sufferings with great eloquence; in refusing to sing theirs Vigny and Leconte de Lisle had used equal eloquence and had merely reversed the medal. (Nothing, as their contemporary Sainte-Beuve remarked, so resembles a hollow as a swelling.) Rimbaud's determination to use suffering, self-consciously, as a means to an end, leaves his Romantic predecessors, even if not the Romantic language, far behind.

Surely the ordeal does not have to be literally painful for it to be useful to the poet. Until we know a great deal more about Rimbaud than we do now, and than we seem likely to learn, we may not take his poetics to require the active experience of discomfort. Enough, for his purposes, and ours, if he thought of it as real and if, through the enactment of it, he did attain to the visionary state which we call that of an *Eidetiker* — and which he called the Unknown.

But our doubts about the literal authenticity of his suffering justify raising one further question: did discomfort necessarily *precede* the vision? All of the means Rimbaud himself suggests or that his interpreters imagine him using to achieve the visionary state — including alcohol, drugs, tea or coffee, vigils, and masturbation — would seem to involve some kind of euphoria, however momentary. And each of them conducts, at its own pace, to exhaustion. However much Rimbaud sounds as if the sufferings came first, it should be emphasized that it is after the euphoric instant that the consequences of excess become unpleasant. It is true that he feared that his enterprise would end in failure and this seems to imply that the vision itself may turn out to be more than his mortality can bear. But, looking closely at the words of the "Lettre du voyant," what he actually says is that the thing to be feared is the loss of the vision's meaning: "et quand, affolé, il finirait par perdre l'intelligence de ses visions." This could, and probably does, mean that the stimulus may wear off, the vision depart, and the poet be left uncertain as to what he has seen.

Whoever heard of a poet, Rimbaud or any other, who found the quintessential instant of creation anything but pleasant? For all the paradise is artificial, it is still a paradise. Such, in deference to those who insist that Rimbaud's experience is somehow mystical, is also the experience of the mystic. Aridity may be hard to conquer, but when eventually the mystic attains the state of contemplation, his condition is one of bliss. In the case of a poet, the same condition is called epiphany.

If Rimbaud's experiment looks back to Blake, Coleridge, Hugo, Baudelaire, and their like, it also looks forward to the work of men like Proust and Joyce and the others who have testified to there being those moments of extraordinary, irrational perception, in the life of a poet, when a sort of grace is vouchsafed him to see things as they really are beneath their outward appearance. These are Proust's "privileged moments," Joyce's epiphanies. Their distinguishing characteristic, the vision—whether seen in dream or trance—seems more real to the beholder than anything in waking, normal life. Rimbaud's poetic process could, if successful, result in the experience of similar states.

The attentive reader of the "Lettre du voyant" realizes that there before his eyes it has already done so, in the figure of the wood finding itself metamorphosed into a violin, analogously to a man who discovers himself a poet. As the paragraph proceeds, the reassociations shift and re-form themselves again: from violin he becomes a whole orchestra. But at the same time as he is the orchestra he is also the conductor, holding in his hand, however, not the baton (here the transformation assures him an even greater sense of fulfillment) but a violin bow with which he produces mighty music. This music is eventually identified as his own poetry.

Whether he knew what he was doing or not, Rimbaud had recorded an epiphany.

So far as his poetry itself was concerned, the process he had discovered guaranteed its freshness, for here was a method for renewing old materials; he had little access to new ones, and he was dreadfully short on real, personal experience. The process of disassociation and reassociation takes care of the difficulty, for however old the materials themselves, the reassociated image will be his own. But though the advantages afforded the poetry may seem the central issue to readers who live a century later, they may not have been of ultimate importance to Rimbaud.

It may have been of much greater consequence to him that he had now identified his pursuit of happiness with the practice of poetry itself, the effort toward euphoria with the effort of creation, and the record of the euphoric vision with the poem. Some of his previous writing had already hinted at this possibility: in the fugue poems the separation of happiness and poetry is inconceivable.

And if the object of his fugues was felicity, then he had found an acceptable substitute. Physical flight up hill and down dale, at this point so effectively frustrated by his mother, could be replaced by a fugue of the imagination, and thus the combination of freedom, nature, and love was still accessible. He had found a way, which no one could ever bar, of getting out of Charleville. It is doubtful if poetry had ever before been put to so welcome a purpose.

Yet, even at this triumphant juncture, there are ominous portents. It is not merely that the "Lettre du voyant" expresses the apprehension of failure, born of his realization of his own inadequacies, and the peasant shrewdness which reminded him occasionally that he was, after all, a very *petit bonhomme*; the letter also reveals the weak point in his whole formula. For it is evident in the very first of his recorded epiphanies, the one just mentioned in which he sees himself simultaneously as musician and as mighty orchestra—so that the music seems to come from him but be symphonic—that the image is subject to constant metamorphosis. His epiphany is, so to speak, in motion. And if felicity is somehow to be connected with a brilliant and euphoric (possibly eidetic) image, what will happen to happiness if, in the long run, the image refuses to remain steady for his delighted contemplation?

Poetry is now indeed the way to happiness, but this sort of fugue, like the others, is doomed to eventual defeat.

Chapter V — The Poem as Fugue

"Le Bateau ivre" has been the subject of an incredible amount of comment, not all of which has been useful for the elucidation of the poem. An assiduous search for sources has shown that Rimbaud had probably read Jules Verne, Chateaubriand, Poe, and numerous others whom it would have been entirely normal for a youth of his age and education to read in any case, and has proved what we knew very well in the first place, that never having seen the ocean himself Rimbaud had to get his information from people who had had the opportunity to do so. Such information would be more helpful had Rimbaud been intent upon turning out a manual for navigators; it can be positively a hindrance if it obscures the fact that the ocean upon which the errant boat embarks is one no sailor ever saw and that by nature this poem is an account of a vision—

into which, doubtless, went such reminiscences of secondhand sea lore as happened to have clung in his mind. In spite of Izambard and Verlaine, the wonder is not that the poem was written by a poet who had never looked upon salt water; it would have been a wonder if, knowing anything about salt water, he had written such a poem.

The poem is a narrative. Something or someone, who speaks in the first person, glides down "impassive" rivers to tidewater, and then for ten nights (and presumably days) is tossed about by the tumultuous waters of the open sea. The experience is a joyful one, and at the end the speaker has a feeling of freedom and purification. Now begins a new experience, which lasts for months, during which, either *in* the sea or *upon* it, the speaker actually sees what other men have thought they glimpsed from time to time—and there follows a catalogue of the wonders of the sea. But there comes a moment when the "I" who is speaking is tired of, or unequal to the vision, and wishes to return to ordinary life again. Straightway he is at home, looking back upon his experience, and being sorry that he cannot renew it. The only water in Europe which attracts him is the shallow pool where a child (perhaps himself) is sailing a paper boat on a spring evening. But he no longer has the strength, or the courage, to resume his visionary voyage.

Such, reduced to prose and relieved of its detail, is the story told by "Le Bateau ivre." Most critics grant that the account is an allegory. The events of the narrative on the whole are such as could happen to a boat that had gone adrift, but the speaker has human emotions, and there are a few events that would be meaningless unless they happened to something, or someone, other than a boat.

Allegory from a poet leads inevitably to extravagance from critics, and it is easy to understand, as a natural reaction, the position of those who, weary unto death of interpretations that make "Le Bateau ivre" an adumbration of Rimbaud's whole career (including the years in Abyssinia), prefer to take the poem for a "Parnassian" parade of brilliant images. To leave matters at this stage, however, would be to recognize no meaning in the poem other than the overt one, abandoning the last four stanzas entirely, passing over much of the narrative as hopeless mishmash, and radically reducing the dimensions of the poem in general. Critically, such a solution is unsatisfactory. But it must also be admitted that accepting the poem as allegory is not in itself a better solution. Allegory it is, indeed, but allegory of what?

In other words, the identification of poet and boat, so that the story told by the poem may be understood in application to both, is clearly central but also bristling with difficulties. No few attentive readers have felt the poet's story to be one of undergoing some sort of *rite de passage*. At the beginning he is young and inexperienced; his trip over the waters would be the acquisition of the experience and would effect the transformation from adolescent to adult; the final stanzas would embody the recognition that adulthood, once achieved, is not finally satisfactory and that childhood, or else a return into the experience itself, would be preferable to it. Such an understanding gives aid and comfort, especially, to interpreters who have been led by parts of *Une Saison en enfer* to think that the motive behind much of Rimbaud's poetic behavior was a desire to return to a golden moment of childhood. The weakness of such a reading is that, taken in the light of the central equation of poet with boat, it simply does not hold up. Three passing references—to children and sour apples, to the "deafness" of the infant brain, and to showing the large golden fish (*dorades*) to children—are hardly persuasive, and the lovely image at the end of the poem, of the child at evening sailing his toy boat over a small pool, can be very easily explained without appeal to the *rite de passage* hypothesis: it can as easily refer to a return to ordinary prosaic experience after an extraordinary poetic one. Moreover, however much the boat may become fouled and waterlogged in its navigations, it surely does not set out upon them as a young and pristine vessel; it has been doing its share in a workaday world.

For this is not just any craft whatsoever. The poem emphasizes the mediocrity of this "bearer of Flemish wheat and English cotton." It is a canal barge, hauled by horses along a towpath, such as a boy could see any day along the Meuse or on the neighboring canals. Such a humble, even vulgar, vessel would strike a French child as an unpicturesque and humdrum feature of the normal landscape. It is quite true that, since Petrarch, numerous poets had equated themselves, in one way or another, with boats, but there is a vast difference between Rimbaud's equation and one like Baudelaire's, "Notre âme est un trois mâts cherchant son Icarie." A three-master spells romance and adventure; the destination of Rimbaud's barge is some dull cargo wharf in a basin at the junction of two artificial waterways. One of the major implications of the poet-boat metaphor is that, given the nature of the boat, what happens to the poet can happen to anybody—or, more specifically, that the most arresting visions may be vouchsafed to the least extraordinary humans. This consideration in itself is enough to preclude taking "Le Bateau ivre" to be a poem about growing up.

On the other hand, the analogy between this metaphor and the one which appears both in the letter of May 13 to Izambard and in the "Lettre du voyant" is inescapable. "So much the worse," the poet had written, "for the wood that awakes to find it has become a violin," or for the metal that discovers itself to be a trumpet. As wood is to violin and normal man to visionary poet, so again is cargo carrier to the craft with the privileged destiny. That the poem is about a transformation is clear, but rather than a transformation of youth into man it is one from the ordinary to the extraordinary.

2

Comme je descendais des Fleuves impassibles,
Je ne me sentis plus guidé par les haleurs:
Des Peaux-Rouges criards les avaient pris pour cibles,
Les ayant cloués nus aux poteaux de couleurs.

J'étais insoucieux de tous les équipages,
Porteur de blés flamands ou de cotons anglais.
Quand avec mes haleurs ont fini ces tapages,
Les Fleuves m'ont laissé descendre où je voulais.

Dans les clapotements furieux des marées,
Moi, l'autre hiver, plus sourd que les cerveaux d'enfants,
Je courus! Et les Péninsules démarrées
N'ont pas subi tohu-bohus plus triomphants.

La tempête a béni mes éveils maritimes.
Plus léger qu'un bouchon j'ai dansé sur les flots
Qu'on appelle rouleurs éternels de victimes,
Dix nuits, sans regretter l'œil niais des falots!

Plus douce qu'aux enfants la chair des pommes sures,
L'eau verte pénétra ma coque de sapin
Et des taches de vins bleus et des vomissures
Me lava, dispersant gouvernail et grappin.

The equivalence of poet and boat is not, we should notice, specified at the beginning of the poem. What happens until we are at least halfway through the fifth stanza is a series of events which can be accepted as happening literally to a boat. No double understanding is necessary. The craft has slipped down the "impassive" rivers after its towmen have been picked off by the Red Indians. It has finally come to the tidewater it has wanted to reach. There it has bounced about joyously for ten nights. Finally the green waters have entered the hull, cleansed it, and swept away rudder and anchor. That it should have felt the need of being clean, of getting rid of the "stains of blue wine and of vomit," is the first intimation that everything in the poem will not fit into a narrative that remains always on the level of literalness.

But the water carries away not only the soilure but also the rudder and anchor. These names have a place in the ordinary marine vocabulary, and we finish the stanza feeling that if the allegory has wavered toward inconsistency, it has done so only for a moment. And in addition, we have been alerted for the most important lines of the poem, which follow directly:

Et dès lors, je me suis baigné dans le Poème
De la Mer, infusé d'astres, et lactescent,
Dévorant les azurs verts; où, flottaison blême
Et ravie, un noyé pensif parfois descend;

Où, teignant tout à coup les bleuités, délires
Et rhythmes lents sous les rutilements du jour,
Plus fortes que l'alcool, plus vastes que nos lyres,
Fermentent les rousseurs amères de l'amour!

Je sais les cieux crevant en éclairs, et les trombes
Et les ressacs et les courants: je sais le soir,
L'Aube exaltée ainsi qu'un peuple de colombes,
Et j'ai vu quelquefois ce que l'homme a cru voir!

"Le Poème/De la Mer" merits special attention. In ordinary French, and in poetry earlier than Rimbaud's, one would emphasize the word "mer," and the inference would be that the sea is *as wonderful as* a poem. But Rimbaud has capitalized both substantives, as if to draw special attention to them, and manipulated his prosody to bring both words under heavy stress. "Poème" occupies the most conspicuous position, occurring at the final and figuring in the rhyme. But the line runs over, so that the principal word of the *rejet*, "Mer," would normally receive heavy stress also. In fact, the conventions of traditional versification would make the stress on "Mer" heavier than that on "Poème," since the effect of *enjambement* is to transfer some emphasis from the end of the verse to the end of the *rejet*; especially when the phenomenon occurs at the end of the first verse of a couplet, the ear hears nothing it recognizes as a rhyme word and has only the rhythm to tell it that the end of the line has been reached. But it is not clear that Rimbaud intended to stay within the tradition. He had fallen into the habit of frequent *enjambements*, as a cursory inspection of the previous months will show. Hence, even though this is the first instance of it in this particular poem, the run over of the thought can hardly be said to compel the reader's attention as it would if the poet were one who made less abundant use of the device. It is thus plausible to read the lines as if "Poème" and "Mer" were of equal value. The additional fact that the poet capitalizes both words makes this reading seem, all in all, the most appropriate.

The reader now finds himself contemplating a metaphor in which the element of *as-if* (the dawn *as if* a pilgrim in russet mantle clad) has been largely replaced by an assertion of identity. The Sea *is* the Poem; the Poem *is* the Sea. In the terms of the allegory this amounts to an almost mathematical statement: the Sea is to the boat as the Poem is to the poet. And here again we are using the terms of the "Lettre du voyant," because here, as in the letter, the poem is not something which the poet creates but something, rather, which he attains. The letter consequently becomes an instrument for deciphering the allegory.

The identity of the "Fleuves" down which the boat glides

toward the sea must remain problematical, but the first two stanzas repeat the element of a descent, as if toward slumber. (Note that one *falls* asleep; the identification of falling with loss of complete consciousness is commonly reported.) It is equally clear that the speaker has wanted this to happen. The "haleurs" which the Redskins have taken for targets would have to be whatever forces had kept him from the descent and taken him off in some other direction. Their fate is one that Rimbaud would not have denied the agents of constraint who surrounded him in Charleville—his mother, the Church, his bourgeois neighbors, and the rest. Once they have been overcome by whatever has made him unaware of them—the Redskins are thus identical with whatever has brought him to the borders of the trance—noise is replaced by quiet and the poet finishes the first stage of his progress *toward* the poem.

It seems obvious that the boat's first taste of the sea should be equated, in the allegory, with the poet's first experience of the poem. But it appears also that up to here something has inhibited him. The wild course of these ten nights has been a joyful one, but the sensations involved have been those of movement—far more meaningful for a boat than for its human counterpart. It is only when the water rushes into the hull to wash away the wine stains and the vomit, and at the same time to sweep away rudder and anchor, that they become dazzlingly visual. Does this mean that this soilure is for the poet what rudder and anchor mean for the boat?

It may seem at first that only a negative answer is possible; the marine equipment named is inevitably associated with the notion of control and it is difficult to see anything of the sort in the other symbols. But, on further reflection, control is to be associated with the normal function of boats; riding at anchor and steering are parts of everyday reality. And we have Rimbaud's word for it that a part of *his* everyday reality, during the weeks when this poem must have been composed, was dedicated drinking; he was trying to be as much of a bum ("s'encrapuler") as possible. The wine stains, moreover, are characterized in the poem as "taches de vins bleus," and *bleu* here has a special meaning. *Vin bleu* is also known in France as *le vin qui tache,* which will not wash out of a table cloth, the cheapest kind of acrid wine, literally with tones of blue in its color, which Frenchmen drink only in the last extremity. (Investigators have since established a one-to-one ratio between increase in its consumption and the progress of alcoholism in France.) In view of Rimbaud's finances—his mother was keeping him "without a copper"—it is more than probable that such wine was what he was drinking in quantity. If this was the case, the word "vomissures" needs no commentary. His report to Izambard that his "sufferings" were "enormous" may be taken to bear this out. The mess which had to be washed away, as were also the rudder and anchor, is the last reminder of life along the Meuse. After this cleansing he is detached from his home world, and completely free so that the vision may begin. This vision is the Poem which is also the sea, and we have heard his triumphant cry: he has seen what others have only glimpsed.

And now comes what may best be described as an inventory of wonders:

> J'ai vu le soleil bas, taché d'horreurs mystiques,
> Illuminant de longs figements violets,
> Pareils à des acteurs de drames très-antiques
> Les flots roulant au loin leurs frissons de volets!
>
> J'ai rêvé la nuit verte aux neiges éblouies,
> Baiser montant aux yeux des mers avec lenteurs,
> La circulation des sèves inouïes,
> Et l'éveil jaune et bleu des phosphores chanteurs!

J'ai suivi, des mois pleins, pareille aux vacheries
Hystériques, la houle à l'assaut des récifs,
Sans songer que les pieds lumineux des Maries
Pussent forcer le mufle aux Océans poussifs!

J'ai heurté, savez-vous, d'incroyables Florides
Mêlant aux fleurs des yeux de panthères à peaux
D'hommes! Des arcs-en-ciel tendus comme des brides
Sous l'horizon des mers, à de glauques troupeaux!

J'ai vu fermenter les marais énormes, nasses
Où pourrit dans les joncs tout un Léviathan!
Des écroulements d'eaux au milieu des bonaces,
Et les lointains vers les gouffres cataractant!

Glaciers, soleils d'argent, flots nacreux, cieux de braises!
Échouages hideux au fond des golfes bruns
Où les serpents géants dévorés des punaises
Choient, des arbres tordus, avec de noirs parfums!

The reward of the Promethean poet, Rimbaud had said in the "Lettre du voyant," would be to bring back knowledge of a kind never previously vouchsafed to men. It would appear from the inventory we have just seen that knowledge was synonymous with particularly brilliant vision.

He had said also that if the *voyant* "sees form" he will "bring back form": and these six stanzas are organized as firmly as a public oration, in an anaphora which piles each declaration upon a previous one, building toward a climax. Each of the first five ends with an exclamation point which marks a step in the mounting excitement. The propositions are complete; each flows into the next in the series: "J'ai vu," "j'ai rêvé," "j'ai suivi," "j'ai heurté," and again "j'ai vu." Then, in the sixth stanza, an exclamation point replaces a comma in the enumeration, which, even so, hurries on to another exclamation at the end of the quatrain; the rhythm has accelerated. And here at last the anaphora breaks, as if syntactically complete propositions can no longer adequately bear the burden, and the language indeed becomes ejaculative: "Glaciers, soleils d'argent, flots nacreux, cieux de braises." However many of the images in this third movement of the poem have been "borrowed"—given Rimbaud's age and experience they could hardly be anything else—the tension and excitement are his own doing, built by him into the structure of the poem. That he never could have seen them in factual reality is less important than that they should have returned from the storage of memory to be seen with a vividness to which generations of readers have testified. Whether or not a psychologist would have classified him as an *Eidetiker,* such images are the kind that textbooks describe as eidetic—so brilliant that they seem to be projected into objective space where they may be contemplated, as if detached from the imagination.

And this has been the poetic experience, the "Poème de la Mer" in which he has been "bathed." It has been entirely visual, a fact which will have bearing upon Rimbaud's later development: it is the eye which has been enthralled by things seen in and on a miraculous sea, under all possible lights, in all latitudes, amid all sorts of fantastic sea life, past menacing reefs, flowery islands, sargassos, and glaciers. The detail of the vision has been studied repeatedly and need not be re-examined here. What has been less often noted is that in this part of the poem the voice hardly speaks for the boat as well as the poet; the allegory has been almost completely suspended; the passage can be read as involving only a series of wonders and the eye which beholds them.

But now the tempo slows and the allegory emerges as the presence of the boat is again felt.

J'aurais voulu montrer aux enfants ces dorades
Du flot bleu, ces poissons d'or, ces poissons chantants.
— Des écumes de fleurs ont bercé mes dérades
Et d'ineffables vents m'ont ailé par instants.

Parfois, martyr lassé des pôles et des zones,
La mer dont le sanglot faisait mon roulis doux
Montait vers moi ses fleurs d'ombre aux ventouses jaunes
Et je restais, ainsi qu'une femme à genoux . . .

Presque île, ballottant sur mes bords les querelles
Et les fientes d'oiseaux clabaudeurs aux yeux blonds.
Et je voguais, lorsqu'à travers mes liens frêles
Des noyés descendaient dormir, à reculons! . . .

For these three stanzas the boat lies quiet in the water, rocked gently by slow swells, almost an island, a perch for sea birds covered by their droppings. The dominant image in them shows a hulk sunk so deep in the water that, indeed, like Verne's "Nautilus," it may at times be moving below the surface. But two images evoke much less the boat than the poet: the reference to the "martyr of the poles and zones," and the other about "remaining like a woman on her knees." A feeling of fatigue and quiescence has succeeded the excitement of the previous part.

Exactly what the passage adds up to with reference to the narrative — the poem seen as the report of a series of events — is blurred by the factor of time. The state of quiescence is represented as recurrent by the adverb "parfois" ("Parfois, martyr lassé des pôles et des zones"), with the implication that there have been alternations of excitement and repose, but in the tonal composition of the poem there is no blur: quiescence replaces excitement, and once excitement has died down it does not return.

Excitement has ceased to be in order, for there is no longer a present vision. It is seen now in retrospect:

Or moi, bateau perdu sous les cheveux des anses,
Jeté par l'ouragan dans l'éther sans oiseau,
Moi dont les Monitors et les voiliers des Hanses
N'auraient pas repêché la carcasse ivre d'eau;

Libre, fumant, monté de brumes violettes,
Moi qui trouais le ciel rougeoyant comme un mur
Qui porte, confiture exquise aux bons poètes,
Des lichens de soleil et des morves d'azur;

Qui courais, taché de lunules électriques,
Planche folle, escorté des hippocampes noirs,
Quand les juillets faisaient crouler à coups de triques
Les cieux ultramarins aux ardents entonnoirs;

Moi qui tremblais, sentant geindre à cinquante lieues
Le rut des Béhémots et les Maelstroms épais,
Fileur éternel des immobilités bleues,
Je regrette l'Europe aux anciens parapets!

Here again the movement is organized into a single, periodic sentence and again an anaphora gives additional emphasis. The speaking voice now identifies itself clearly as the boat, both by direct statement ("Moi qui, bateau perdu") and by suggestion ("Qui courais, planche folle"). More of the detail of the sea vision is inventoried, and perhaps in even greater splendor than before. The boat now contrives to move in a third dimension: having previously navigated upon and under water, here it goes off into the ether, also, as its freedom reaches something of an apotheosis. But all this is being recalled from a past that is over and finished. The experience has come to an end. The verbs fall into an imperfect ("trouais," "courais," "faisaient," "tremblais") unrelated to any perfect; instead they take their orientation from a present tense of the principal verb: "Je regrette l'Europe aux anciens parapets!" Thus their meaning is that he who was doing these things is doing them no longer, and the impact of the principal verb creates a note of self-recrimination. It is possible to read this long, marshaled period as the announcement of a failure.

For the cargo boat this means a return from sea to the old, familiar rivers with their stone retaining walls and parapets. For the poet it means that his vision has been abandoned in favor of tedious, repressive everyday reality. This is the end of the adventure; there remains only the speaker's exhaustion.

> J'ai vu des archipels sidéraux! et des îles
> Dont les cieux délirants sont ouverts au vogueur:
> – Est-ce en ces nuits sans fond que tu dors et t'exiles,
> Million d'oiseaux d'or, ô future Vigueur? –
>
> Mais, vrai, j'ai trop pleuré! Les Aubes sont navrantes.
> Toute lune est atroce et tout soleil amer:
> L'âcre amour m'a gonflé de torpeurs enivrantes.
> O que ma quille éclate! O que j'aille à la mer!
>
> Si je désire une eau d'Europe, c'est la flache
> Noire et froide où vers le crépuscule embaumé
> Un enfant accroupi plein de tristesses, lâche
> Un bateau frêle comme un papillon de mai.
>
> Je ne puis plus, baigné de vos langueurs, ô lames,
> Enlever leur sillage aux porteurs de cotons,
> Ni traverser l'orgueil des drapeaux et des flammes,
> Ni nager sous les yeux horribles des pontons.

Whereas the other movements of the poem have been carefully organized and coherent, this one is not: the stanzas are so little related to each other that they might properly be separated by lines of dots, and two of them do not cohere internally. In brief, a kind of disintegration has taken place.

The emotional tone varies also. The third and fourth stanzas are much quieter than those about sidereal archipelagos and painful dawns; the voice is calmer, the utterance less fragmentary. The poem ends with the speaker caught between unacceptable alternatives: he is too marked by his experience to return to normal life, and the last word of the poem introduces a new symbol of restraint, for *pontons* were prison hulks. He is back where he was before the green water washed him free.

3

Despite the wide variety of the interpretations which this poem has inspired, there would seem to be very little doubt, once attention has fallen upon the pattern, that the events of the "Bateau ivre" follow the general shape of the fugues Rimbaud had actually attempted. A sudden departure toward an unspecified but deeply desired goal is followed by a euphoria in which everything is lovely and pure delight; this turns eventually to a quieter, if still deep, pleasure—as if some of the original impetus had been spent; and then comes the inability to continue and the necessity of going back to a life which one does not want and which means nothing. These moods are not entirely unfamiliar to us: the vision of the sea in the "Bateau ivre" goes with emotions which are similar to, though less intense than, those in "Ma bohème"; there is a parallel between the calmer mood which follows it and the one of "Les Chercheuses de poux," a poem whose subject is generally conceded to be the gentle treatment given Rimbaud by the aunts of Izambard when the boy turned up in Douai, much the worse for travel, toward the end of his second escapade; and the frustration in which the story ends is expressed by only too many of the poems Rimbaud had written during the winter in Charleville. We are once more dealing with a poem about running away from home.

We are also dealing with one about euphoria, and here again the territory is familiar: the constituents of his felicity are those we know about. Freedom is again the prerequisite: beatitude does not establish itself until all the agencies, and even memories and reminders, of restraint have been removed. And the delight that begins when freedom is complete is delight in a spectacle of nature—in the form of an ocean more wonderful than ordinary mariners could possibly imagine. Love is also clearly present, in association both with the inception of his vision and with his inability to put himself back into the special state of grace once the joy and excitement have passed. All this serves to identify the author of the "Bateau ivre" as the one we know already. What is different here is that now he is involved with perfection—total freedom to enjoy a nature which leaves nothing to desire, a bliss which other men may have glimpsed or thought they did, but which has now been *known*.

Numerous details in the poem are best understood if it is recognized that, movement by movement, it follows the prescriptions of the "Lettre du voyant." Clearly, the Redskins at the beginning represent whatever means he used to throw off the feelings of control and restraint which bind one to normal life. And the reference to wine and to a love stronger than alcohols makes one suspect that these were intoxication and masturbation, used to achieve the willed and reasoned disordering of the senses which the letter has made famous. The preliminary experience of bouncing about for the ten nights, during which no vision is vouchsafed to him, sounds very much like the ordeal hinted at in his correspondence: it is represented as joyous but strenuous, and at its end the final restraints are removed. The third movement is the experience of voyancy itself: at long last he *sees*. And the brief fourth movement records the moment of great and holy calm that follows the first rapturous excitement. The fifth records the failure, foreseen in the letter, when the *voyant,* having attained his vision and knowledge, proves unequal to it and falls back. And finally, the concluding stanzas announce the frustration and weakness of him who has been forced to leave the prosecution of his quest to other horrible workers.

Added to this, there is also the fact that the vision itself does have the hallucinatory nature assumed in the letter. It is true that only one image in the section actually pictures a hallucination as such—the often quoted reference to the eyes of panthers which bear human skins. But the whole strategy of the vision is to bring together phenomena that are in themselves familiar but in juxtapositions that, to say the least, are new and strange. We have all seen rainbows, for example, and bridles, and schools of fish; even so, using rainbows to bridle schools of fish is something beyond the scope of normal, unhallucinated consciousness. All in all, the "Bateau ivre" fits the specifications of the letter so well, and illustrates it so aptly, that one finds only one reason for Rimbaud's not having copied it down with the other poems which he scattered through the text sent to Demeny: he had not yet written it.

We are not obliged, of course, to believe that this poem is an account of a poetic trance that Rimbaud actually experienced. Internal evidence, actually, points to a different conclusion. The poems that are most clearly the results of a visionary trance—both among the *Derniers Vers* of 1872 and in the *Illuminations*—are characteristically incoherent. The visions themselves appear to be fragmentary and fleeting, and the syntax in which they are reported is equally broken and discontinuous. In addition, the poet regularly speaks as if the reader, who as a matter of fact is left in complete ignorance, is already aware of the substance of whatever may be the object of contemplation. (Rimbaud's treatment of the definite article, which bears particularly upon this assumption, will be matter for discussion later.) In the "Bateau ivre," on the other hand, the vision itself is coherently organized and is relatively stable; the syntax is equally well organized; and the poet is quite conscious of speaking about what he alone has seen. In view of this aspect of the poem, it seems far less likely that Rimbaud is reporting something he has actually been through than what he imagines such an experience to be like — or, rather, what it would have been like had he learned at this juncture how to produce it.

Yet all the same, Miss Starkie's conjecture that Rimbaud was forced to defer his experiments in voyancy until he had left Charleville for Paris, where he could find narcotics, does not fully commend itself, either. There is no question about his having tried narcotics after he had got to Paris. But there is relatively little reference to drugs in the later poetry and very little to encourage inference even from the most eager, whereas alcohol is in the picture from the very first references to voyancy, and talk about the abuse of alcohol figures frequently in the correspondence from that point on. Furthermore, however difficult it would have been for a boy without money to obtain, say, hashish, during the winter of incarceration in a war-isolated provincial town, the availability of cheap wine, if of no stronger drink, is not to be doubted. We do not know what, in the long run, Rimbaud required to put him in the desired state, but the conclusion that alcohol was at least not completely ineffective is inescapable. He could, therefore, have been trying, though perhaps with incomplete success, to put his theories into practice before he left home and as early as the writing of the poem in question.

Thus nothing forbids believing that while he was still in Charleville Rimbaud did at least enough experimenting to get some idea of what the hallucinated state was like. Certainly he could have done so, and it is hard to think that a youth who, from everything we know about his psychological make-up, was rarely disposed to delay putting ideas into action, should have passed up the opportunity. And in turn, the knowledge gained could have served him as a guide for putting together the images that make up the poet-boat's adventure.

One element of mystery remains to plague us, however: why does the vision fail him and why, afterward, is he back in "Europe" and in the state of frustration in which the poem ends? Not that we have not seen ample evidence that Rimbaud was accustomed to the prospect of failure. The phantasy of "Les Réparties de Nina" comes back to cold reality with the sound of the woman's voice in the final line. Poems like "Roman" and "Oraison du soir" show him fully aware of his callowness and lack of stature, not to say out-and-out ridiculousness. Failure is seen as a very real possibility in the "Lettre du voyant." And the shape of "Bateau ivre" is the shape of his literal, physical fugues—departure in joy and excitement, a gradual quieting down, and an ignominious return. But if this poem was a monumental wish fulfillment, as it is here represented to be, was there no further reason why, if the poet were going to indulge himself in a flight from reality at all, he should not have gone all the way and indulged himself in a successful and complete one?

Circumstances save us from having to fall back into pure speculation at this point: what seems likely to have happened in this poem is what, demonstrably, did happen in poems written about a year later, and the question becomes one of whether the condition of Rimbaud's imagination that was responsible had not already established itself.

As has been quite clear from examination of Rimbaud's earlier poems, felicity regularly presented itself to the poet accompanied by, and inseparable from, a play of light. At the triumphant instant when he enters "the Poem of the Sea," which is "infused with stars" and "lactescent," he is surrounded by "green azures" – and this is his first statement of his ecstasy. The "azures" in turn are stained by the "bitter russets." The low sun lights him with rays which seem to have coagulated. Nights are green. There are rainbows. In those moments when he sinks into a completely static happiness, the fish he sees are golden. And when he looks back, after his vision has left him (or he, it) its character is subsumed in the "million of golden birds" – in which lies the possibility of some "future vigor." In the whole catalogue of thronging living things which make up so much of his vision, shapes are barely stated – that is, we know of fish, but what kind out of so many? and of birds, but are they eagles or wrens? – whereas colors are fully specified.

There can be small doubt that this play of light is what most delighted those readers who have considered the "Bateau ivre" to be a Parnassian poem. The imagery is indeed so bright as to dim anything else in one's memory of the poem, and they are of course right so far as the first, somewhat primitive enjoyment of the poem goes: this brilliance is the height of the reader's immediate experience of the work. Later, one realizes that these colors and reflections do not stand by themselves alone, because they also stand *for* the felicity of the poet and are the external correlates of an internal state; they thus have meaning above and beyond what the colors and images of a Parnassian poem are permitted to carry. And they are, accordingly, fragile in the extreme.

Psychologists who have studied the phenomenon of image formation have recognized considerable variation in behavior from individual to individual. Some appear to specialize in images of great clarity and color, and others in images that have shape but no color at all. Some imaginations studied cast up their images slowly, one at a time, and others have almost kinescopic activity, producing images in rapid series, as on a motion picture film, without the subject's exercising any notable control over the flow.

Rimbaud's poem itself is adequate proof of the presence of color in his imagination. It would appear also that he belonged to the category of image makers whose images followed each other rapidly. We know nothing, naturally, about their actual rate of flow, but if anything is clear about the "Bateau ivre" it is that the poem works with a stream of images which succeed each other and upon none of which it attempts to dwell. No particular principle seems to govern the order of their appearance, none is seen more than once, and there is no recorded effort to call one back once it has been seen. Each is a fleeting presence before the mind's eye. And his frustration at the end of the poem arises from a felt inability to renew his contemplation of them.

Had his early experience already taught him that the process of stimulating the flow of such images, brighter and truer than life so long as they lasted, also guaranteed their invincible transiency? The one dependable characteristic of any such stimulation is that eventually the stimulant loses its force. Certain lines near the end of the poem, particularly hard to understand otherwise, take on plausible meaning in the light of such a hypothesis. Any dawn may properly be qualified as "navrante" if it sees the moment of emerging from alcoholic stupor, just as any sun that rose upon a hangover would be "amer." One can easily imagine how the moon of any such night would, in retrospect, appear "atroce." And if it is the case that a further stimulant was furnished by sexual exhaustion, it is not surprising that at the night's end "l'âpre amour" should have filled him with "torpeurs enivrantes." Certainly the implication that the vision ended because the stimulant had run its course is not to be rejected out of hand, especially since it also offers an explanation of the vision's breaking off as it does in the poem with the speaker's wish to return to the ancient parapets of Europe. From the beginning of the poem down to this point, it will be remembered, the poet-boat is entirely passive. Everything that happens, happens *to* him. Even his will is too feeble to form a wish: note the tense of "j'aurais voulu montrer aux enfants ces dorades." The wish to return to Europe thus constitutes a first reawakening of the will, a return from sleeplike trance to waking reality; and the event ceases to be an arbitrary one, and becomes, in addition to the turning point in the narrative which it has always appeared to be, an easily understandable one.

Thus the artificial fugue which Rimbaud sketched in the "Lettre du voyant" and then described in the "Bateau ivre" turns out to contain an inherent fault: the escape is only momentary. And the transiency of the state—we have at least strong reason to suspect—is due to the instability of the imagery of happiness. The poem is, it has been alleged, *about* a poem (and thus self-reflexive in a way one attaches to Mallarmé sooner than to Rimbaud). It is this poem within the poem which holds our attention especially, because it is also his vision of happiness—the happiness which has always been his central subject. Those he will write later will most often be like it, except that they will be this central poem alone, unaccompanied and unsupported by the other material, and less coherent and intelligible exactly because they are not so accompanied and supported.

They, too, will contain the identical flaw—which turns out to be at the same time the flaw in Rimbaud's poetic process. The image, lovely though it may be, will not remain, and without its brilliance everything will be even darker than before.

Chapter VI – The Tortured Heart

IT WOULD have been in character if Rimbaud had enclosed some samples of his new, hallucinated poetry with the "Lettre du voyant." He was not, as we know, temperamentally disposed to hide his achievements, and he valued the opinions of Demeny as well as of Izambard. In addition, Demeny was older than he, familiar with his enthusiasms, and thus not unlikely to take his momentous news with a grain of salt. Some demonstration of what he could do would seem to have been particularly in order, since his letter is a declaration that, as poets, his friends have taken the wrong track and he alone knows the right one. One of the great mysteries about the "Lettre du voyant" is his failure to offer anything of the sort.

The three poems he copies into his text for Demeny are from the hymns of hate he had written during the winter, and as far from being hallucinated as one could imagine: the farewell to love of "Mes petites amoureuses," the brutally realistic "Accroupissements," and the political satire called "Chant de guerre parisien." The three have been noted here as characteristic of his habit of lashing out, when things went wrong, at whatever displeased him. His eye, in "Accroupissements," is extremely severe in its detailed accuracy. The others share its tone of violence. His language is harsh, increasingly obscene, perhaps intentionally unpleasant.

One rereads them with new interest, spurred by Rimbaud's request that Demeny burn all previous manuscripts and the inference that the new texts reflect a major change in his poetry. They do reflect a change, as we have seen — but not the one we are looking for. One shortly renounces the search for any sign of hallucination, or for any other evidence of his putting the theories of the letter into practice, in the conviction that there is less chance of finding such here than even in those written before the winter of 1870–1871. Never, it would seem, was there a less hallucinated poet.

At the end of his letter to Izambard, on the other hand, appears one text extremely unlike those in the letter to Demeny. His words about it convey no notion that he intends an illustration of the theory of poetry he hints at in the preceding paragraphs: "I give you this: is it satire, as you say? Is it poetry? It is phantasy, anyhow. — But, I beg, don't do any underlining, with a pencil or even mentally." And after the text he adds: "This is not meaningless." The poem was "Le Cœur supplicié"; later copies would bear alternative titles, "Le Cœur du pître," and "Le Cœur volé."

Mon triste cœur bave à la poupe,
Mon cœur couvert de caporal:
Ils y lancent des jets de soupe,
Mon triste cœur bave à la poupe:

Sous les quolibets de la troupe
Qui pousse un rire général,
Mon triste cœur bave à la poupe,
Mon cœur couvert de caporal!

Ithyphalliques et pioupiesques,
Leurs quolibets l'ont dépravé!
Au gouvernail on voit des fresques
Ithyphalliques et pioupiesques.
O flots abracadabrantesques,
Prenez mon cœur, qu'il soit lavé!
Ithyphalliques et pioupiesques,
Leurs quolibets l'ont dépravé!

Quand ils auront tari leurs chiques,
Comment agir, ô cœur volé?
Ce seront des hoquets bachiques,
Quand ils auront tari leurs chiques:
J'aurai des sursauts stomachiques,
Moi, si mon cœur est ravalé:
Quand ils auront tari leurs chiques
Comment agir, ô cœur volé?

If the dates assigned by Mouquet are right, Rimbaud could perfectly well have included this poem in the "Lettre du voyant." Whatever his reason, he did not do so. Yet eventually this turns out to be the only poem of those associated with the letter that he submitted to *both* his friends. One is tempted to suspect that at first he did not know, himself, whether his performance in "Le Cœur supplicié" was connected with the experience of voyancy or not, but that, as time went on, he became more and more aware of such a possibility. In any case, it was not one of the poems he wrote down once and then forgot: when he writes Demeny again, on June 10, not having had an answer to his previous letter, he encloses a copy of the poem. His specific request for a reply to the "Lettre du voyant" suggests that he was more than mildly curious about his friend's reaction to his ideas. It is true that in the same letter he has copied out "Les Poètes de sept ans," and "Les Pauvres à l'église," neither of which would seem to be connected with the subject of voyancy. But of the three poems, "Le Cœur supplicié" is the only one to which is attached a note of explanation, with, at its end, a "Voici — ne vous fâchez pas —" which may be less a warning against anger than a plea for understanding.

Such facts do not justify our concluding that this is an early, and perhaps the earliest, example of poetry written according to the formula of the *voyant,* but they do emphasize Rimbaud's feeling that the piece was different from the other writings his friends had seen. This alone would make it merit special examination. And its hallucinated nature turns out to be attested by an ambiguity, entirely alien to what he had written up to this time, which later resulted in a most curious, and long enduring, disagreement among his interpreters. Critics have rarely contrived to vary so radically as to what a poem is about. And it happens that, for once, amid all the heat there shines a new light on the nature of a poem.

The controversy started with the early efforts of Paterne Berrichon to keep his brother-in-law's name and memory respectable. No hand to stick at an absence of documentary proof, Berrichon had decided that Rimbaud must have run away from home one more time than was on the records. How else explain this particular poem? The flight, he reported, had taken place on or about May 15, 1871, and thus put Rimbaud in Paris at the height of the Commune. According to Berrichon, Rimbaud had not only made the trip but had also witnessed scenes of great violence, attempted to join the National Guard, and even spent some days in the barracks called the Caserne de Babylone. Berrichon affirms that during this time Rimbaud was a bystander at incidents when an undisciplined soldiery got obscenely drunk. As usual with this biographer, the story is substantiated by numerous details which, under scrutiny, prove very difficult either to verify or discredit.

According to him, "Le Cœur supplicié" grew out of this escapade. His dates are of course wrong, but the error did not become apparent until Izambard published the letters—almost entirely preoccupied with poetry—written by Rimbaud from Charleville at the very time when Berrichon puts him in Paris, and in one of which he mentions an "idea" which holds him back when his anger prompts him to leave for the capital. This evidence appeared too late to affect the acceptance of the story, the interval between Berrichon's account and Izambard's having been long enough for a whole folklore to accrete upon the subject.

Ironically for Berrichon, his story ended by making Rimbaud's career look not more respectable but considerably more lurid than it had before he began his embellishing. A whole congeries of critics pondered his tale. They had at hand the one document he had had, the poem. Borne by the original impetus of Berrichon's fiction, and more gifted than he in close reading, they pushed toward the conclusion that Rimbaud had been no merely passive spectator at debauchery. One of the later ones, Wallace Fowlie,* makes the specific statement that "the boy . . . still in his sixteenth year, was subjected to scenes of pederasty, probably in one of the barracks, where he considered enlisting in the army of the Communards. This rape of Rimbaud (either literal or imagined) probably helped to make possible the longer and fuller experience with Verlaine." He later admits that this is an "extreme" interpretation of the poem, but the interpretation remains the one which he accepts.

* *Rimbaud* (Norfolk, Conn.: New Directions, 1946), p. 34.

It is, in fact, not impossible that Rimbaud was in Paris sometime, say between April 18–19 and May 10–11. In other words, there is no day by day evidence that he stayed in Charleville during that time. But neither is there the least shred of evidence that he did *not* stay there. And the only reason on earth for believing that he made the trip to Paris is "Le Cœur supplicié," which must absolutely be the issue of an experience far more traumatic than mere spectatorship at a drunken rout and one which can be imagined taking place only in Paris.

Such legends are manifest boons to interpreters of literature who derive biographical "fact" from poetry and then, reversing the process, interpret the poetry in the light of biography. The traumatic episode that Rimbaud is supposed to have encountered shortly becomes pivotal in his development as poet: his "new" maturity has been won through suffering; his sexual instincts have deviated from shock; he is subject to great throes of revulsion and disgust. This embroidery can continue indefinitely.

Such activities might pass uncriticized if they were based on the only possible interpretation of the poem, but in this case they are not. To Georges Izambard, for example, "Le Cœur supplicié" is about an imaginary experience not in a barracks but aboard a ship. Izambard was a poet himself, knew his Rimbaud as well as anyone, and read without malice—except perhaps for the annoyance he always felt toward the fabrications of Berrichon. He finds the poem full of Rimbaud's haunted feeling for the sea, understands the unpleasant imagery to be associated with seasickness, and, possibly because both poems endow salt water with the property of washing away soilure, proclaims this one to be a forerunner of "Le Bateau ivre."

The variance in these interpretations is wide enough to make one wonder whether the several readers had not been misled by radically variant versions of the texts. This is not the case: there are in fact three versions—Izambard's, Demeny's, and one finally published by Verlaine—but only one difference in reading is relevant to the discussion. Verlaine's version gives for the eleventh line a time of day ("à la vesprée") instead of the reference to a rudder that appears in the other two. It is clear that no critic has been led astray by this divergence alone, so that the seat of the disagreement must lie deeper.

With two important exceptions, all the critics who have dwelt on "Le Cœur supplicié" at length have joined either the proponents of seasickness or those of trauma. Yves Bonnefoy manages not to commit himself. And Jules Mouquet feels that the poem adds up to a generalized expression of discontent and disgust.* The inescapable fact of the matter is that a dispassionate examination of the text itself reveals something to support *all* the views expressed to date.

Logically this should be impossible. In all common sense someone or other must be guilty of misreading. But ordinary logic, and the kind of sense we call common, would be beyond their depth here if a case could be made for the poem's being the first instance in the Rimbaud canon of truly hallucinated poetry. In the circumstances, such a possibility should not be rejected out of hand.

Characteristically, Rimbaud furnishes no help toward understanding what he has written. His letter of June 10 to Demeny is possibly a bit more communicative than the one he wrote on May 13 to Izambard. This poem, he explains, is the antithesis of those in which cupids play foolishly about and hearts take the air, decorated with flames, green flowers, damp birds, Leucadian cliffs, "etc."—in other words, not one posed against a background of sentimental *louisphillipard* claptrap. One could have welcomed something more.

* Yves Bonnefoy, *Rimbaud par lui-même* (Paris: Editions du Seuil, 1961), p. 42. Mouquet's opinion is in his notes on the poem in the Pléiade edition; he also summarizes the other positions taken in the controversy.

Unless one reads into them what one hopes to find, the two letters reveal hardly more than that the poet does not expect his friends fully to understand or approve of the new poem and feels that he must warn them of his seriousness. But it may be noteworthy that wanting his poem to get serious attention is not the equivalent of saying that it refers to some unnerving and perhaps disastrous experience. In writing Demeny previously, Rimbaud had deprecated his own efforts. Subsequently he had no reply regarding them. He may now be saying only that he meant what he said before about no jokes and no paradoxes. We can learn more, if anywhere, only from the text.

2

The poem is built around the presiding image of the heart, presented in the first line and kept before the reader throughout. The Freudian suggestion that this is not a heart at all but a representation of the virile member may be rejected, not alone because Rimbaud had not had the privilege of reading Freud, but also because the subordinate imagery does not support such a reading; the heart about which it clusters has to be taken for a cardiac organ if the full import of the central image is to reveal itself; and in addition, taking the poem to be an expression of a castration complex would make the third stanza absolutely unintelligible.

The identity of the heart is unveiled gradually as the first verse progresses. "Mon triste cœur" sounds like a neutral and very shopworn synecdoche, but is rescued from total banality by the concrete and unexpected verb, "baver"; to drool is a physical act and whatever performs it is highly likely to be physical also. And the adverb of place that ends the line contributes another physical detail: the setting is the afterdeck of a ship.

Rimbaud's strategy here is quite familiar—even though the logic of the heart's activity and of the setting resist explanation

— from having since been popularized by the Surrealists. *Seeing* the heart exuding some liquid on the planks of a deck is no harder than *seeing* an eye staring out from the center of a fried egg. In both examples what is missing is the key to the logic of the juxtaposition. But, unlike the Surrealists, Rimbaud suppresses the key only temporarily: three lines from the end of the poem he will make the logic fully explicit. Until then, however, the significance of his image cannot be fully grasped and the momentary effect upon the reader is the one that a Surrealist image produces: a violent disorientation and a confusing inability to put back together a world which has been wrenched apart. In other words, we are exposed to something which conforms exactly to our earlier definition of hallucination.

But at the end of the piece, when the reader learns that the heart must be swallowed down again, the logic is restored and the hallucination explained away. Anyone who has ever been seasick knows the nausea whose persistence promises that the contents will shortly be followed by container; to vomit up one's inside is a trope doubtless as old as the science of navigation. Rimbaud has merely seized a metaphor, which could well be regarded as too worn for further use, and seen the image inherent in it so vividly that one feels it not as figurative but as literal. The metaphor has been projected into the plane of action, a procedure which the modern reader recognizes as familiar, however unfamiliar it could have seemed to its readers of 1871.

Meanwhile, the poet sets about elaborating the image by a process which will eventually enlighten the reader and bring him out of suspense into full recognition of its original, and intended, import. "Caporal," in line two, is shag tobacco, and how the heart comes to be "covered" is clear if we admit that since the most plausible reading of "jets" in the third line involves spitting, "soupe" must be accepted as meaning tobacco juice. The subject of the verb in the third line, "ils," asserts the presence of the spitters, who will be identified in the fifth and sixth as the "troupe" who laugh and joke. At the end of the stanza the dramatic situation is completely stated.

The second stanza sets forth the causes of the heart's discomfort. Obscene and priapic jokes, such as might amuse young soldiers—*pioupiou,* the stem of *pioupiesques,* is derogatory—have "depraved" the heart. This word, like *ithyphallique,* is bound to loom large in any interpretation that assumes the poem to be a report on actual experience. In sober fact, however, all that can be said for certain about *dépravé* is that in this context it establishes a sort of equivalence: what the tobacco juice has done to the heart on a physical plane the jokes have done to it on a moral one. The relationship of tobacco juice and jokes thus becomes one more metaphor to be added to the others.

This equivalence is immediately extended further: the poem next adds the item of the *fresques,* to which the same adjectives are applied as to the ribald laughter. Just what these drawings—if they *are* literally such—may be is a subject for speculation. In Verlaine's version, the one given here, they are on the rudder, and, presumably, already drawn. But what *gouvernail* meant to Rimbaud is beclouded by his vagueness—already evident in the "Bateau ivre"—about the anatomy of ships. Most probably he meant the area aft, along the taffrail, where the steering of a boat is done. Littré accepts this meaning of the word, and it had better be accepted in view of the difficulty for even the merriest of Merry Andrews of expressing his libido on the rudder itself. The variant appearing in both the Demeny and the Izambard manuscripts presents even more difficult problems. "A la vesprée ils font des fresques," leaves a puzzle as to the meaning of "font." This could indicate that the subjects are drawing the pictures, an activity which does not seem particularly plausible in view of the weakness of the light implied in "vesprée"; or "font" could be taken as the equivalent of "play the role of." The "voit" of Verlaine's manuscript helps little in determining which of these other two possibilities would bring the variant readings closer together; it admits either. The divergence between the readings is such as to give one trouble imagining what made the poet substitute one for the other, and one wonders whether the line was not a *cheville* in the first place, and one so completely a filler and so completely not inevitable, that Rimbaud forgot what he had written in the first copy before he wrote out the second and the third. Doubtless we shall never know the answer. It is at least clear, however, that the *fresques*—modified by "ithyphalliques et pioupiesques" as are the ribald jokes also—extend to three the number of outrages by which the heart is beset.

The poem continues, calling upon the waves to cleanse the heart, and here again there is ambiguity. The adjective applied to them, "abracadabrantesques," may imply that they possess a special magic, obtainable through the repetition of some formula. Or it may equally well imply that they are absurd and meaningless. It is impossible to say with confidence whether this is a hopeful or a despairing cry—although in view of the tone of the third stanza, despair would probably be the likelier emotion.

But in spite of the ambiguity, the total meaning of the poem begins to emerge; we begin to find confirmation of the readings of the earlier lines which until now have necessarily remained tentative. Since the washing of the heart is called for as much by the fact of its having been "depraved" by ribaldry as by the splashing with tobacco juice, the relation between the joking and the physical soilure becomes clear. Also, the appearance of "chiques" in the first line of the third stanza supports the identification of "soupe" with tobacco juice. And the sixth line, where the reader learns that the heart must be swallowed again, with renewed nausea, finally reveals the logic of the opening line of the poem: there is now no question as to *why* the heart is driveling on the deck.

3

It should be obvious at this point that only an interpreter convinced beforehand of the rightness of his view could adopt one understanding of this poem and dismiss the other completely. Anyone else will face the inconvenient fact that there is something to be said for, and something against, each.

The general feeling of nausea, the image of the heart vomited upon the deck, the fact that there *is* a deck, the reference to tobacco juice (the plug being the recourse of sailors when the smoking lamp is out), and the availability of cleansing water — to perform the function salt water performs in the "Bateau ivre" — are all relevant to a poem about the sea. But it is a rare sea poem which refers to a ship's crew as a "troupe," or attaches to mariners an adjective like "pioupiesque."

On the other hand, much of the material can be understood as applying to a scene in a barracks, especially if a certain amount of free association is admitted. Words like "caporal" and of course "troupe" have military overtones; "soupe" is army jargon for meal; a "pioupiou" is a soldier. Especially if the line about frescoes is taken to mean that the bystanders, no less than their jokes, are "pioupiesques," there is a substantial amount in the poem which is better explained by what might be called a "military" as opposed to a "maritime" reading. But there is still no bilking the fundamental ambiguity of the poem. Why "poupe" and "gouvernail" if the scene is a barracks? Why "pioupiesques" and "troupe" if it is a ship?

The truth can only be that the divergent reports have been based upon an assessment of the imagery, exclusively, at the expense of everything else a poem includes. The testimony of verse form, rhythm, and language is clear.

If the imagery fails to confirm either of the conflicting readings, the versification argues directly against both. In his letter to Demeny, Rimbaud refers to "Le Cœur supplicié" as "these triolets." This is the only evidence of any interest he may ever have had in any such intricate pattern of recurring lines. He seems to be testing his technical adroitness. And the reader's pleasure in the anticipated return of identical lines is in tune with the real gaiety of the piece. The triolet was never a form designed for the spontaneous outpouring of strong emotions: the obvious planning of the recurrences leaves little room for a feeling of spontaneity. And few forms could seem to lend themselves less readily to expressing sheer distress over an encounter with physical brutality or with seasickness in a degree involving acute physical suffering. Even the most determined defender of any hypothesis which assumes physical, traumatic experience would have difficulty defending at the same time the use of a form which cannot but suggest that the poet's attention is divided between his suffering and the movements of a very complex juggling act.

Evidence furnished by studying the rhythm is similar. The first line ends with a rapid, almost tripping run: "Mon tri′/ste cœur′/ ba′/ve à la pou′/pe." The second is evener and more regular: "Mon coeur′/ cou vert′/ de ca po ral′." The third reproduces this smoothness: "Ils y lan′/ cent des jets′/ de sou′/ pe." But the fourth returns with the tripping energy of the first. This, because of the pattern in which the lines recur, sets the rhythmical arrangement of the entire stanza. The second stanza becomes downright playful. The first line has the tongue dancing over unstressed syllables: "I thy phal li′/ques et piou pi es′/ques" with a slight secondary stress on "piou" because of the exhaustion of the breath. This cadence happens to carry the same stresses as the once familiar ribald song which begins, "Il y avait un moine blanc." If this line, which in the triolet turns up three times, gives the muscles of the tongue something approaching the pleasure of the dance, how is one to describe the pleasure produced by: "O'/ flots'/ a bra ca da bran tes'/ ques"? Perhaps it is enough to say that wherever the rhythms of the piece become specifically suggestive, they suggest anything but trauma.

Such interpretations of the emotional connotations of the rhythm are necessarily subjective and thus not decisive in themselves, but the rhythm combines in turn with an adventurous use of language. The very words that are used to create the most markedly dancelike rhythms are, to say the least, unexpected in a poem. "Ithyphallique" finds its normal context in scientific prose. "Pioupiesque" and "abracadabrantesques" are arrantly coined *ad hoc.* To be sure, in the spring of 1871 Rimbaud is still in the phase where he loves to use unusual words for their own sake; Verlaine will dissuade him from the habit, as well as from his habitual obscenity, some months later. But even at his most venturesome with words, Rimbaud does not elsewhere use his vocabulary to destroy the mood which he is otherwise clearly striving to create in his poem, and it would be idle to pretend that he were doing so here.

The obvious disagreement between the meanings which are allegedly to be found in the imagery, on the one hand, and the testimony of form, rhythm, and language on the other, has the value of pointing toward a possible alternative interpretation of the whole poem. What the imagery offers, in spite of its inherent ambiguity, is an expression of strong though not clearly specified disgust. Disgust *such as* might be represented by seasickness, and even disgust *such as* might follow mistreatment in a barracks, he had already orchestrated adequately in earlier poems of the same year which we know. Here the disgust is tied to a less specific cause, rather than to the atmosphere of the church, for example, or to the behavior of librarians, and becomes in a more direct way the subject itself. There had been much that winter which could turn his stomach—French: *soulever le cœur*—and take the heart out of a man. He seems not to have settled firmly on a title; the adjective varies with each version—"supplicié," "du pître," "volé"—so as to throw emphasis in one case on its suffering, in another on the clownishness of the possessor, and in the third on his feeling of having been wronged. None of the three instances forces us to posit an actual, specific experience; a winter spent in Charleville could, for a Rimbaud, justify any or all.

But we have also to remember that, though disgust dominates the imagery, through the playfulness of the form the poet is setting up a kind of counterpoise to his own discomfort such that tone and image are set off against each other. The resultant contrast produces a wry irony, which becomes a part of the piece's meaning also. Rimbaud has not lost his perspective. He is a poet, to be sure, and one outraged by what has happened to him; but he is also, simultaneously, the realistic youngster who is capable of seeing himself as others see him and who knows that in such a perspective too dramatic a gesture will not fail to look out of place. After all, the only reason that he has had to undergo this unpleasantness is that he has not proved able to break away, and stay away, from his mother. In the "Lettre du voyant" he had been the self-conscious performer who could also arrest his conductor's baton, suspending the performance. The same performer is the ironist of "Le Cœur supplicié," whose irony is a welcome outlet, no doubt, for his feelings and perhaps the only one, an irony seated deep in the matrix of the poem itself, in the contrast between image and rhythm, "content" and "form."

4

Such a reading has at least the merit of accounting for all the major aspects of the poem. But obtaining a reading for the one individual poem seems less important than what the poem shows us about the development of Rimbaud's general poetic practice. The fact that two groups of attentive readers should have varied so widely in their reading reveals the presence of two reference systems in the piece and three possibilities for the reference of any given image: some are found to refer only to the maritime experience, some to the barracks one only, and a number can very possibly refer to either or both. This phenomenon would attract our interest anywhere we found it. It happens that we find it in what may possibly be the first poem Rimbaud wrote after the discovery registered in the "Lettre du voyant," and in what is certainly the poem which was most on his mind when he broke the news to his friends. *And the presiding image of the piece is one which meets the definition of hallucination.*

There is nothing new about hearts or the decks of ships; the new element is the unexpected juxtaposition, which puts a heart where one never was before and creates the strangeness of the poem. Whether or not Rimbaud was consciously applying the new method, we would have to note the effect of strangeness. And we have also noticed that *after the original statement of the hallucination the vision becomes blurred.*

Thus what was suspicion at the moment of reading the "Bateau ivre" here approaches being a conviction. The image-making function of his mind seems to have developed a marked degree of autonomous activity, to have ceased to work under full, conscious control. We have always known, of course, that something compulsive has been at the genesis of many poems, as, for example, a compulsive rhythm was the beginning of Valéry's "Cimetière marin." The behavior of Rimbaud's imagination would appear to be comparably irrational, but the effect of the irrationality entirely different. The image, once seen (and stated) does not remain; it blurs and gives way to others until eventually the visionary, or hallucinative, experience wears out and comes to an end.

Knowing this provides a key for some of the poems he wrote a year later, which are among the most lovely and the most mysterious he ever wrote.

Chapter VII – The Unstable Image

NOT ALL of the poems Rimbaud wrote during the spring of 1872 are lovely. Some – like "Honte," which merely documents the rapidity with which his relationship with Verlaine deteriorated – are anything but that. But all, without exception, are mysterious. Not even the most devoted reader feels that he has forced them to give up their entire secret. Like some music, they seem to mean more than they are capable of saying. None of the earlier poems, not even "Voyelles" with its dizzying whirl of images, produces quite the same impression.

"Voyelles" belongs to the same general moment, and mood, as the "Bateau ivre." If the number of attempts to elucidate a poem were the measure of its success, this one must surely rank – with the "Bateau ivre" – among Rimbaud's most successful. It has mystified many, perhaps because their elucidations, several of which are little short of ingenious, regularly proceed from the assumption that there must absolutely be *some* reason why a given letter should call up the associations it does in the sonnet. The interpretations, from one proposing that these associations were suggested by a child's ABC, to one that the poem repeats an alchemist's formula, all take for granted a hidden rationale which may be found if we but search enough; the idea that the poet's imagination has no choice but to behave responsibly is widely accepted. Few critics welcome the possibility that what the poem says has no meaning beyond the overt one. That the vowel A should be black and associated with fuzzy flies just because the poet feels it to be so — in other words, black and fuzzy only because black and fuzzy — is a notion which tends to paralyze critical activity. Yet when one simply reads the poem without appealing to preconceptions, the chance that Rimbaud's imagination was playing a gratuitous game seems considerable.

We resist such a solution in the case of "Voyelles," as in all the other poems written before his definitive escape from home, because Rimbaud gives such a strong impression of being able to say exactly what he intends to say. Nothing in form, syntax, or vocabulary suggests that he has given up hope of communicating with his reader or hearer — with someone somewhere outside his own ego. But such a suggestion is omnipresent in the poems of spring, 1872 — those labeled in the Pléiade edition as *Derniers vers.* It is largely responsible for the difference of our critical disposition toward the *Derniers vers,* as contrasted with the one we take toward the mysteries of "Voyelles" and other pieces of its period.

Earlier, his syntax had been noteworthily firm and continuous; now, in 1872, sentences are frequently incomplete, conjunctions are missing, ellipses are everywhere; discontinuity is the rule rather than the exception. His incoherence reminds us of certain inchoate passages in the "Lettre du voyant," rather than of the poems like the "Bateau ivre." His once solid versification gives way: *enjambement* is so common that in some of the pieces the feeling of reading or hearing verse almost disappears because the ear hardly hears the line stops, and because the poet is so manifestly inattentive to such conventions as the alternating of masculine and feminine rhymes. At times he gives up rhyme entirely part way through a poem and completes it in unrhymed verse. The impression is inevitable that either Rimbaud no longer cares or else his poetic faculties are partly paralyzed.

2

Yet the change, however much it disorients the reader at first, is actually much less extensive than it seems. Beneath the differences, the behavior of the imagination remains essentially the same. His familiar preoccupation with his own happiness continues to inform the major part of what he writes. Love and freedom may have become minor themes temporarily, but the experience of nature compensates by acquiring even greater importance for him than before. Poetry continues to represent for him an activity indistinguishable from the search for epiphanies. And, although this search is often rewarded, we are as always conscious of an undertone of apprehension: he goes on being haunted by the possibility of defeat.

It seems doubtful whether the spring of 1872 was particularly happy for Rimbaud. There may have been a first, fine, careless rapture following his escape from home, because he now had the liberty he had so much wanted. His idyl with Verlaine, whatever else may be said about it, gave him a kind of love: we may as well face the fact that, a great popular belief to the contrary, a poet's life is not necessarily his noblest poem — the purest poetry rises sometimes from the impurest sources.

Vitalie Cuif Rimbaud had not been one to waste affection on her sons, and compared with what he had known in Charleville, Rimbaud's situation in Paris may have seemed to him the good life. But for how long?

His behavior in Paris was not that of a happy youth. It is not merely that he forsook the principles of the catechism: by all accounts the Rimbaud of 1872 was an odious little creature, busy laying the foundations of an unenviable reputation. He was openly and aggressively offensive even to the associates who had befriended him. He lived parasitically on his friends, absorbed as much absinthe as he could, experimented with narcotics, tried to knife a companion, paraded his homosexuality, and broke up Verlaine's marriage. Legends of his obscene behavior may be exaggerated, but cannot be complete fabrication. He had written Izambard the year before that he intended to become a ne'er-do-well; it sounds as if, in the interval, he had carried out the program to the letter. He was outrageous and there is a compulsive aspect to his outrages; one suspects them of being products of anxiety and obsession. In the jargon of our moment he would be called "disturbed."

Nor does the poetry of this season sound any happier than the biographical circumstances would lead us to expect. This juvenile delinquent, with his deviated tastes and possible homicidal tendencies, was writing some poems which, for lyric depth and poignancy, and perhaps also for their ability to elude precise comprehension, may be mentioned in the same breath with Shakespeare's songs. Not all are sad, by any means; "Eternité" and "O saisons, ô châteaux" are unmistakable epiphanies of felicity. But most of the nineteen pieces which form the collection are far from speaking of happiness. His poisonous wrangling with Verlaine echoes in "Honte," and melancholy is plainly audible in "Comédie de la soif." The burden of others, including "Bannières de mai" and "Mémoire," is that felicity is transitory and uncertain, ready to slip through one's fingers and leave the whole enterprise of poetry a failure.

Surely it was not a happy man who wrote "Chanson de la plus haute tour":

> Oisive jeunesse
> A tout asservie,
> Par délicatesse
> J'ai perdu ma vie.
> Ah! Que le temps vienne
> Où les cœurs s'éprennent.

But however precarious happiness may seem, contact with nature is no less part and parcel of it. The contact must have been, almost exclusively, an imaginary one—so clearly so that we are perpetually faced with the question whether, in the complexity of Rimbaud's responses to life, feeling happy automatically produced the thought of being outdoors or whether—a complete alternative—the thought of nature automatically induced the thought of happiness. In any case, the Rimbaud of 1872 is an enthusiastic nature poet at a time when his experiences of nature were few indeed.

Rimbaud was living in Paris and feeling the discomfort of late-spring and summer heat. The rooms he lived in—there were two, in succession: he had only one at a time—were small, and one of them was tucked away under the eaves of a house in one of those mansards where students and domestic help have sweltered for generations. One poem of the period, "La Chambre est ouverte," appears to describe just such a crowded situation. Given what we know about the scantiness of his finances and the nature of the quarter he lived in, it is certain that he was a victim of nineteenth-century urbanism. Yet, except for the poem above noted and one other of which we may not be sure, his imagination frequents not the city but a smiling countryside.

From his Paris garret he imagines rivers, ponds, sands, bridges, hills, flowering fields, open sweeps of grass, willows, poplars, nut trees, briars. One poem takes him into farming country where there are fruit bushes, and the phantasy "Entends comme brame" involves peas growing in a mist. Whereas earlier nature had been holy and not to be profaned (for example, by war and death), now at times she also becomes a symbol for health and a kind of purity. In "La Rivière de cassis," the stream rolls, to be sure, through strange valleys, and is associated with revolting mysteries involving dungeons and the dead passions of wandering knights, but the crows have the voices of angels and the wind in the tops of the fir trees is good; the passer-by will take courage when he sees the birds; the crows even have the salutary power to drive away "the wily peasant who clinks his glass," an ominous figure who is obviously an enemy of happiness. Crows had appeared — "chers corbeaux délicieux" — in his poetry the year before; now they have become almost talismanic.

A similar symbolism pervades his other phantasy on alcohol, "Comédie de la soif." First the speaker's grandparents, back from the grave, urge him to take to drinking good dry wine in the open air — "au soleil sans imposture" — then cider and milk, and finally tea and coffee. Identifying themselves as peasants, they also urge him to contemplate nature.

> L'eau est au fond des osiers:
> Vois le courant du fossé
> Autour du château mouillé . . .

In the next section the Spirit speaks, invoking the "Eternal Undines," Venus, "the Wandering Jews of Norway," and the "dear, former exiles," urging them, respectively, to "part the fine water," "stir the pure wave," "tell of the snow," and "tell of the sea." Apparently the sea retains here, and shares with the snow, the purifying power it had in the "Bateau ivre" and "Le Cœur supplicié."

Now come his friends and urge on him the rivers of beers and ales which come tumbling from the mountains. And to their proposals, as to those of his peasant grandparents, he replies with sharp refusals. The grandparents end their first appeal to him with a question: "Que faut-il à l'homme? boire."

His reply rejects the answer "boire" and substitutes going off to die "by barbarian rivers." When they finish telling him to drink cider and milk, his rejoinder refers not to what they have just said, but to the original question about what man needs; what is needed, he says, is to go "where the cows drink." And in response to their proposal of tea and coffee he returns still a third answer to the other question: needed is to "dry up these buckets of tears." ("Tarir toutes ces urnes" is a variant upon "pleurer comme des urnes"; the expression is used also by Flaubert in *Madame Bovary.*) These sane and healthy drinks which the grandparents advocate are again rejected at the end of the second section of the poem, after being associated with sea and snow, the purity symbols which the Spirit mentions.

> Non, plus ces boissons pures,
> Ces fleurs d'eau pour verres;
> Légendes ni figures,
> Ne me désaltèrent;
> Chansonnier, ta filleul
> C'est ma soif si folle,
> Hydre intime sans gueules
> Qui mine et désole.

These lines are less hermetic than perhaps they seem. The first two verses reject the drinks commended by the grandparents; the second pair dismiss the images proposed by the Spirit: none of these will overcome his thirst. The identity of the "chansonnier" in the fifth line becomes clear if we remember the title of the poem: "Comédie de la soif." This is indeed a play and these are players who have been appearing on the stage—except that the figure originally called Spirit now is addressed as a cabaret singer. The thirst "which eats away, and saddens," is clearly the opposite of natural.

Now the "friends" appear on scene and speak of wines, bitter, and finally absinthe, all beverages which cause drunkenness and the contrary of those appearing earlier in conjunction with the purity of nature. These also the "moi" rejects:

> J'aime autant, mieux, même,
> Pourrir dans l'étang . . .

The "Poor Man's Dream" which is the fourth section repeats the pattern of proposal and rejection. The first nine verses contemplate escape from the predicament through travel—the possibility of drinking quietly and dying happily in some old city, north or south. This also is refused: it would mean giving up the pleasure of intoxication.

> Et si je redeviens
> Le voyageur ancien,
> Jamais l'auberge verte
> Ne peut bien m'être ouverte.

The fifth and concluding section, however, returns to an explicit vision of nature as well as to another vision of death. Of the four ways of dying contemplated in the poem—death by the "barbarian rivers," death in the scum of a pond, death in a foreign city, and now death "among damp violets"—only the last, to die in the dew amid violets at dawn, does not repel him.

Such juxtapositions of nature and death images are new to the reader, and lead to the suspicion that Rimbaud had come to a rather desperate pass. He was, in biographical fact, drinking heavily, could not bring himself to stop, and may well have wondered how the debauchery would end. To the extent that the voice in the poem is the voice of the poet and not of an occasional persona, Rimbaud does indeed sound wretchedly insecure. Even to die amid nature's violets is still to die, and the image of himself decaying in one of nature's ponds surely does not suggest comfortable adjustment to a world which is forever fresh and green and new.

The same juxtaposition of nature and death images turns up also in "Bannières de mai," toward the end of the first stanza, and recurs in the second:

> Aux branches claires des tilleuls
> Meurt un maladif hallali.
> Mais des chansons spirituelles
> Voltigent parmi les groseilles.
> Que notre sang rie en nos veines,
> Voici s'enchevêtrer les vignes.
> Le ciel est joli comme un ange.
> L'azur et l'onde communient.
> Je sors. Si un rayon me blesse
> Je succomberai sur la mousse.
>
> Qu'on patiente et qu'on s'ennuie
> C'est trop simple. Fi de mes peines.
> Je veux que l'été dramatique
> Me lie à son char de fortune.
> Que par toi beaucoup, ô Nature,
> — Ah! moins seul et moins nul! — je meure.
> Au lieu que les Bergers, c'est drôle,
> Meurent à peu près par le monde.
>
> Je veux bien que les saisons m'usent.
> A toi, Nature, je me rends;
> Et ma faim et toute ma soif.
> Et, s'il te plaît, nourris, abreuve.

Rien de rien ne m'illusionne;
C'est rire aux parents, qu'au soleil,
Mais moi je ne veux rire à rien;
Et libre soit cette infortune.

Here the conjunction is all the more interesting because this poem contains an authentic epiphany, one of those divine moments of perception when everything is transcendently right, and in harmony; the sky is beautiful "as an angel," and in communion with the sea. Here, for an instant, he feels placed outside of time like Proust's narrator upon discovery of his private access to the past. At this moment of insight, in Rimbaud's case, there is also a reconciliation with death. The poem tends to confirm the feeling that at this time Rimbaud was unhappy: he would like to be less "lonely" and less "a nullity." But, simultaneously, he can accept death in nature if such is his destiny. His felicity would appear to be the result of the application of his method: he speaks in the second stanza of patience and ennui, and of "peines"—which can be read as a synonym of the "souffrances" mentioned in the "Lettre du voyant."

Rimbaud's placing this poem in a group—a rare instance of his arranging his own work—under the title *Fêtes de la patience* may be extremely significant to us. "Patience" implies not only waiting but also a kind of persistence; taking into account the context of *patienter* in "Bannières de mai," the import of the title may be that all these poems are fruits of the process described in the letter. In other words, each may embody an epiphany.

That there is an epiphany in "L'Eternité" seems almost certain.

Elle est retrouvée.
Quoi?—L'Éternité.
C'est la mer allée
Avec le soleil.

Ame sentinelle,
Murmurons l'aveu
De la nuit si nulle
Et du jour en feu.

Des humains suffrages,
Des communs élans
Là tu te dégages
Et voles selon.

Puisque de vous seules,
Braises de satin,
Le Devoir s'exhale
Sans qu'on dise: enfin.

Là pas d'espérance,
Nul orietur.
Science avec patience,
Le supplice est sûr.

Elle est retrouvée.
Quoi? – L'éternité.
C'est la mer allée
Avec le soleil.

Here again the awareness of time is suspended and a conjunction of nature has taken place – sea and sun have joined. Once more there has been waiting – the soul is a sentinel. Waiting – "patience" – is linked with knowledge; we remember that knowledge was to reward the poet of the "Lettre du voyant." And waiting is also associated with suffering, for which he now uses a very strong word, "supplice."

If the word "Là," which begins the first line of the fifth stanza as well as the third line of the third, is taken to refer to the imaginary locale of the epiphany, and the "braises de satin," in the fourth stanza, is read as alluding to the light effect when sun and sea meet, it would seem clear that with what Emily Dickinson would call "a certain slant of light" has come a feeling of release and freedom in which hope and prayer have become irrelevant.

We are not required, of course, to believe that the feeling arises from a literal and ecstatic experience of nature. Actually, the process may be the entire opposite: when the feeling in question is induced by any of the means Rimbaud has at his disposal, an image involving nature may automatically accompany it. The rule holds that nature is inseparable from his notion of felicity.

Individual readers may detect the presence of an element of epiphany in other poems of this group. I should, myself, claim to find one in "Chanson de la plus haute tour," in which the familiar "patience" has led to the eventual disappearance of fears and sufferings. But the presence is not easily demonstrable, for there is too clear a note of discouragement and defeat in the poem.

> J'ai tant fait patience
> Qu'à jamais j'oublie;
> Craintes et souffrances
> Aux cieux sont parties.
> Et la soif malsaine
> Obscurcit mes veines.
>
> Ainsi la Prairie
> A l'oubli livrée,
> Grandie, et fleurie
> D'encens et d'ivraies
> Au bourdon farouche
> De cent sales mouches.

The figure of the "Prairie"—his waste land—may not be dismissed. The two versions of the poem vary considerably:

even the refrains of the text Rimbaud quotes in the "Alchimie du verbe" chapter of *Une Saison en enfer* are very different from those in the text of 1872. But the sense of both versions persists: he has wasted life "par délicatesse," and through too much "patience" he has become like a neglected field full of weeds and of buzzing, dirty flies. In the "Alchimie du verbe" he likens himself as poet, we remember, to a drunken fly buzzing about the urinal of an inn. "Chanson de la plus haute tour" records a feeling of failure.

But this poem is not a failure itself—nor are the others of these *Fêtes de la patience*. From our angle, he was wrong to condemn them in "L'Alchimie du verbe" as examples of his aberration. As is true of many poets, he was a poor judge of his own work, regularly too severe. But it is noteworthy that what he later disparaged most in these pieces was the tone. He disliked the sadness which now moves his reader so deeply.

Yet the sadness is genuine enough; and his disliking it suggests the nature of the failure. He always identified poetry with happiness—in a very real way poetry had failed him, and he was left paying the cost of his artificial *dérèglement raisonné de tous les sens* which the writing of the poetry entailed. He could occasionally achieve an epiphany, but this was not enough.

What was the cause of the failure? We cannot be exactly sure, of course, but there is no small possibility of its being something already affecting the behavior of his imagination in "Le Bateau ivre" and "Le Cœur supplicié." His images of felicity, like all his images, tend to dissipate as he contemplates them.

3

Two of the poems of 1872, "Mémoire" and "Larme," dramatize this dissipation itself, and a third, "Michel et Christine," derives its structure from the metamorphoses of images.

"Mémoire" lends itself to varying interpretations because of its convoluted syntax as well as of the shifting of its imagery.

I

L'eau claire; comme le sel des larmes d'enfance,
L'assaut au soleil des blancheurs des corps de femmes;
la soie, en foule et de lys pur, des oriflammes
sous les murs dont quelque pucelle eut la défense;

l'ébat des anges; – Non . . . le courant d'or en marche,
meut ses bras, noirs, et lourds, et frais surtout, d'herbe. Elle
sombre, avant le Ciel bleu pour ciel-de-lit, appelle
pour rideaux l'ombre de la colline et de l'arche.

First, the "clear water" and then an impression of blinding whiteness, likened to the dazzlement caused by the salt in children's tears – it is as if the eye had started from the stream's surface to look higher, into light progressively stronger and more blinding. Immediately the syntax becomes complex and difficult; if Rimbaud is purposely dislocating his word order, as Mallarmé does, we should understand: "The assault of the whiteness of the women's bodies in the sunlight." There is no possibility, in any case, of understanding the whiteness to be "as if of" women's bodies, since the genitive *des* makes us take the bodies as concrete images. Yet we shall not see these particular females again; they merely begin a succession of references to women in the poem. And the sun, in subsequent stanzas, will be associated with the image of an eye. Thus these first two lines set up ambiguities of which there will be later echoes.

Next the image is replaced by one of oriflammes, in large numbers and – the French admits either reading – the color of lilies or else with the figures of lilies worked upon them. These are placed under "the walls some maid defended."

The beginning of the second stanza leaps on to another

image which seems to be substituted for the one of knights thronging below battlements: the "frolic of angels." Possibly the reference to the second female intruder in the poem, Jeanne d'Arc, justifies the association of angels, but the point is hardly relevant in view of what follows.

For the poet now cries "No" — and rejects the image, returning to "the golden current moving." And with this identification of the water as a stream, the meaning of the first stanza opens out. We are on the bank of a stream; the battlements seen through the blinding light are the stone retaining wall along the bank. Something at its foot — but what? — has evoked the image of oriflammes, which, by etymology, are the color of gold. It is probably a flower of some sort, in numbers such as make possible the suggestion, and yellow in color.

Since the *souci d'eau,* or marsh marigold, plays such an important role in later stanzas that the poem would be incomprehensible without it, and has the further advantage of being yellow, it seems the likely choice. Only one thing is wrong with it: there is little about a marsh marigold to suggest the pennon of a knight. But there is a white aquatic flower, the water renunculus, which sometimes blossoms so thick on northern French streams that the total effect is as if a white cloth had been laid upon the surface and were undulating with the current like the silk of oriflammes; it would do, except that the color is wrong. Have images of the two flowers contaminated each other? In any case, the knights are crowded out by the frolicking angels — who may even have been suggested by the flashing of color alone.

Abruptly the poet brings himself back to the present reality. But as soon as his eye returns to the water's surface his imagination is again diverted, to the form of still another female, this time dark, with arms which are heavy, black, and "especially" cool, formed by the grasses of the stream bed as they move with the current, lying as if in a bed which requires the sky for a canopy and the shadows of hill and bridge for curtains.

Obviously this is a moment of felicity. Nature has joined with eroticism. With the beginning of the third stanza her bed becomes a marriage couch and the water she lies in is golden. Rimbaud has used gold before (see "Le Bateau ivre") as a symbol for something infinitely desirable. For the poet, the whole point of living is to retain images like this.

II

Eh! l'humide carreau tend ses bouillons limpides!
L'eau meuble d'or pâle et sans fond les couches prêtes.
Les robes vertes et déteintes des fillettes
font les saules, d'où sautent les oiseaux sans brides.

Plus pure qu'un louis, jaune et chaude paupière
le souci d'eau – ta foi conjugale, ô l'Épouse! –
au midi prompt, de son terne miroir, jalouse
au ciel gris de chaleur la Sphère rose et chère.

Momentarily he does retain it, but only momentarily. For the eye leaves the surface and moves to the bank, where either willows stand along the water like young girls in green dresses with figures of birds worked into the material, or else girls stand there as willows would. (The image is somewhat murky.) And along the bank again there is gold, for marsh marigolds fringe the water like an eyelid over an eye suggested by the liquid surface, and the marigold is jealous of the sun, directly above in the hot summer sky.

With the return of gold – and the marsh marigold – to the poem there is also a thought of conjugal faith, and there is no reason for the reader to suspect that the "Spouse" mentioned is anyone but the cool, dark woman of the stream bed. But in the last two verses the image series breaks; the association of marigold with the coin, the eye, and the sun allows the thought of jealousy a place also, the cool, dark, attractive woman of the stream bed disappears and in her stead there enters a cold, black one who looks remarkably like Vitalie Rimbaud.

III

Madame se tient trop debout dans la prairie
prochaine où neigent les fils du travail; l'ombrelle
aux doigts; foulant l'ombelle; trop fière pour elle;
des enfants lisant dans la verdure fleurie

leur livre de maroquin rouge! Hélas, Lui, comme
mille anges blancs qui se séparent sur la route,
s'éloigne par-delà la montagne! Elle, toute
froide, et noire, court! après le départ de l'homme!

The flowers now flashing whiteness from the field are probably wild carrot. Against their whiteness stands out a figure, "Madame," too tall, too proud, trampling the blossoms, thoroughly alive. The previous female figures in the poem have all been pleasant. But in contrast to the maiden of the castle, the girl-willows, and the woman in the stream, this one is not. As so often in Rimbaud's later poetry the condition of the light is spoiled by the intrusion of a foreign element. There will be no further mention of gold except as reminiscence. And whiteness, in the form of a male figure, "Lui," runs away from the woman, over the mountain.

I have no quarrel with readers who remember Vitalie Rimbaud's inability to keep her menfolk at home and take this scene to represent the departure of the father and brothers. Nor do I object to seeing it as referring to Rimbaud's departure alone. What seems to me more important, however, is that the Black Wife is displeasing to contemplate whereas the woman in the stream was pleasing, and that gold has disappeared in a clash of black and white, which in turn resolves in a victory for black at the end of the sixth stanza, as the woman stands watching the flight of the man. In other words, the image of felicity has given way to the image of infelicity. About this much there can be no mistake, and this is the central event of the poem to which all the others, whatever their inherent value, are related.

In the seventh and eighth stanzas the image of the woman in the water, and the accompanying gold, are declared to be irrecoverable. So, too, is the delight that went with them. They are replaced by the sound of the woman weeping below the "ramparts." Only the wind is there to hear the rustle in the poplars; the only moving figure on the flat, dead, reflectionless surface is that of an old dragger, toiling endlessly. The verse moves as slowly as it is possible for French verse to move.

IV

Regret des bras épais et jeunes d'herbe pure!
Or des lunes d'avril au cœur du saint lit! Joie
des chantiers riverains à l'abandon, en proie
aux soirs d'août qui faisaient germer ces pourritures!

Qu'elle pleure à présent sous les remparts! l'haleine
des peupliers d'en haut est pour la seule brise.
Puis, c'est la nappe, sans reflets, sans source, grise:
un vieux, dragueur, dans sa barque immobile, peine.

Thus, after the drama of the Black Wife, we have returned to the river and defeat. Happiness would lie in recovering the image of the woman in the stream, but it is gone except as memory. Once more the metamorphosis has taken place and nothing remains now but to express the ultimate frustration.

V

Jouet de cet œil d'eau morne, je n'y puis prendre,
ô canot immobile! oh! bras trop courts! ni l'une

ni l'autre fleur: ni la jaune qui m'importune,
là; ni la bleue, amie à l'eau couleur de cendre.

Ah! la poudre des saules qu'une aile secoue!
Les roses des roseaux dès longtemps dévorées!
Mon canot, toujours fixe; et sa chaîne tirée
Au fond de cet œil d'eau sans bords, — à quelle boue?

The image of the old dragger is replaced by one of a child, also in a boat, also achieving nothing: the boat is moored too short and merely swings in the current. The water is again identified with the "eye" of the fourth stanza, where it was fringed with marigolds. This flower would appear to be the yellow, "importunate," one; perhaps it is importunate because connected, through its jealousy of the sun, with the intrusion of the Black Wife upon the image of the woman in the water, perhaps also because it represents the gold of felicity which still eludes him. The other flower he is unable to reach is unidentifiable, though one is tempted to take it to be another symbol of felicity. The cry of grief about pollen from the willows is intelligible if related by the reader to the felicity image in the third stanza in which girls and birds and willows are associated. The reference to the "roses des roseaux" is again meaningless botanically (and may mean only that there are now no more pink water lilies among the reeds) but the emotional emphasis is surely upon the fact of their absence, and is unequivocal. The last line of the poem makes clear that where once there was the lovely image of the woman there is now nothing under the ashen water but unlovely mud.

It is common to read this poem as an autobiography, in the sense that central events of Rimbaud's life are treated, lyrically, in it with only a slight effort, if any, at disguise. Good critics have taken it to be a statement that at an early age he was entirely happy, but that his mother's domination later led him to

leave home and that, yearning for his original happiness, he was unable to return to it and was thereby left wretchedly disconsolate. This coincides with certain facts. There *was* a river, the Meuse, near his home where he seems to have played with his brother; his mother *was* repressive; he *did* leave home. But though these items are documented, the rest sounds like fictional biography invented to fit the poem. How do we know?

When the poem is read as an example of the behavior of Rimbaud's imagination, on the other hand, we re-enter territory where footing is surer: the pattern is entirely familiar. Stripped of local, concrete detail it amounts to this: after a moment of confusion the imagination fixes upon an image which either corresponds to, or else causes, a state of euphoria; this image is subsequently crowded out by another which negates it; the euphoria thus dissipates and, like the experience of its correlate image, cannot be recovered; accordingly, the speaker is left in a state of frustration and weakness. What we have is another account of the eternally defeated poetic enterprise; the pattern of "Mémoire" is almost identical with the pattern of the "Bateau ivre," that other poem on the elusiveness of felicity.

If there is a major difference in the two poems taken as imaginative patterns, it is related to the connection between imagery and nature. One of the tendencies originally manifested at least a year earlier has developed radically: nature is light—when the poet is no longer able to find the woman in the water, the fact is that the light has changed. And not only this, what images one forms depends on what the light does to one's eye. In the calculus of this particular poem no causal relationship is suggested. These things are stated as parallel, independent phenomena. The disappearance of the image is not alleged to have come about because of a change of the light. No implication, really, is made as to sequence: the image disappears; the light changes. The sentences are essentially paratactical. But in the two other poems there is stronger reason to feel a cause and effect relation, that is, that the stability of the image which is identified with happinesss is no greater than the stability of nature: the light changes *and* the image dissipates.

4

If only we knew for sure in what conditions Rimbaud wrote the "Alchimie du verbe" text of "Larme," the two versions of this poem would put into our hands a wealth of information about his development. Unfortunately, we have no notion whether the shortening and altering of the later version does not merely reflect a failure of memory. The shorter version changes the position of the speaker—presumably the poet—from squatting to kneeling, makes the interjection of line six clearer by more appropriate punctuation, gives the gourd a color instead of specifying its variety, and changes "the wind, from the sky" to "the wind of God." Such alterations could easily be explained by a desire to revise a poem written some time earlier. But now, most interestingly, the new version goes on to omit entirely the later enumeration of images—"Ce furent des pays noirs . . ."—except for the icicles on the pools. Whether or not Rimbaud had forgotten how the earlier text went, the omissions in the later one emphasize the dramatic situation. The statement is reduced to there having been a scene and a mood, and then a change of weather—light—which swept both away. At the same time, the insistence upon the yellowness, rather than the species, of the gourd inserts a suggestion of gold, and at the end the reference to gold is both explicit and symbolical: "Pleurant, je voyais de l'or—et ne pus boire." Both texts report a picture of felicity momentarily achieved, then lost, and later regretted—and what Rimbaud remembers in 1873, is this, at the expense, perhaps, of the rest.

The longer and earlier text, however, compensates for being less dramatic by being more complete in details which reveal the disposition of the poet.

> Loin des oiseaux, des troupeaux, des villageoises,
> Je buvais, accroupi dans quelque bruyère
> Entourée de tendres bois de noisetiers,
> Par un brouillard d'après-midi tiède et vert.
>
> Que pouvais-je boire dans cette jeune Oise,
> Ormeaux sans voix, gazon sans fleurs, ciel couvert.
> Que tirais-je à la gourde de colocase?
> Quelque liqueur d'or, fade et qui fait suer.
>
> Tel, j'eusse été mauvaise enseigne d'auberge.
> Puis l'orage changea le ciel, jusqu'au soir.
> Ce furent des pays noirs, des lacs, des perches,
> Des colonnades sous la nuit bleue, des gares.
>
> L'eau des bois se perdait sur des sables vierges.
> Le vent, du ciel, jetait des glaçons aux mares . . .
> Or! tel qu'un pêcheur d'or ou de coquillages,
> Dire que je n'ai pas eu souci de boire!

After the image of the drinker disappears, the imagination goes off on a wild, uncontrolled course which does not organize itself into anything particularly intelligible. When this is finished, it returns to the first scene to discover that the original mood has gone for good. Thus both versions recapitulate the story of "Mémoire," but with insistence on different elements. The connection between "Mémoire" and "Larme" is still further emphasized by the presence in the first version of "Larme" of the line: "Tel qu'un pêcheur d'or ou de coquillages . . ." Nothing in the poem itself offers the least plausible explanation of the reference to this fisherman. But at the end of

"Mémoire" there is the sudden glimpse of the old "dragueur" toiling in his boat. Since a fisher for gold or shells would also be dragging the bottom, an explanation presents itself: we recognize the symbol of frustration.

5

"Michel et Christine" is a slightly different case in that the change of mood is not one from elation to dejection, but in it we have the same spectacular transformation of imagery accompanied by a radical change in the disposition of the speaker.

Zut alors, si le soleil quitte ces bords!
Fuis, clair déluge! Voici l'ombre des routes.
Dans les saules, dans la vieille cour d'honneur,
L'orage d'abord jette ses larges gouttes.

O cent agneaux, de l'idylle soldats blonds,
Des aqueducs, des bruyères amaigries,
Fuyez! plaine, déserts, prairie, horizons
Sont à la toilette rouge de l'orage!

Chien noir, brun pasteur dont le manteau s'engouffre,
Fuyez l'heure des éclairs supérieurs;
Blond troupeau, quand voici nager ombre et soufre,
Tâchez de descendre à des retraits meilleurs.

Mais moi, Seigneur! voici que mon esprit vole,
Après les cieux glacés de rouge, sous les
Nuages célestes qui courent et volent
Sur cent Solognes longues comme un railway.

Voilà mille loups, mille graines sauvages
Qu'emporte, non sans aimer les liserons,
Cette religieuse après-midi d'orage
Sur l'Europe ancienne où cent hordes iront!

Après, le clair de lune! partout la lande,
Rougis et leurs fronts aux cieux noirs, les guerriers
Chevauchent lentement leurs pâles coursiers!
Les cailloux sonnent sous cette fière bande!

— Et verrai-je le bois jaune et le val clair,
L'Épouse aux yeux bleus, l'homme au front rouge, ô Gaule,
Et le blanc Agneau Pascal, à leurs pieds chers,
— Michel et Christine, — et Christ! — fin de l'Idylle.

The protest against losing the flood of sunlight is followed in the next line by immediate acceptance. As shadow moves over the scene and the landscape reddens in the new light, the flock of lambs (twice) and the sheepdog (once) are urged to take shelter. Then the metamorphosis of the principal image begins and the sheep are identified with soldiers. In turn this identification is forgotten as the oncoming storm excites the imagination of the speaker, who now sees himself carried off with the wind-blown debris, over "a hundred Solognes," and "over old Europe," "where there will go a hundred hordes." With this last the image of soldiers returns, after an absence of four stanzas, and proceeds to dominate the landscape. The lambs had been the "blond flock" which was equated with the "blond soldiers of the idyl"; now, correspondingly, the horses of the "cavalcade" are "pale." Finally, the image of soldiers changes to that of a single soldier, home from war and seen in domestic bliss, and at the same time the flock of lambs reappears as one single lamb.

Speculation on the procession and the metamorphosis of the images will not overcome all these difficulties, but does open an interesting possibility: the lambs turning into soldiers, the soldiers into a single soldier — who is, indirectly, a metamorphosed lamb himself — the lambs reappearing as one individual lamb and this the Lamb of God, and the ultimate exclamation, "and Christ," leave the figure of Michel strangely blurred. An alternative title might even be proposed: "Christ and Christine." The identification of Michel and Christ would not, of course, be rational: it leaves Michel-Christ lying at his own feet and those of his bride. But this is exactly the point. The other associations in the poem are not reducible to rational logic either. As in "Larme," once the quality of the light has changed the imagination goes off entirely on its own.

The distinction to be made regarding this poem is that here there is no regret expressed for the inconstancy and instability of the imagination. This is the only instance to have appeared in the work so far where Rimbaud is not repeating after Faust: "Verweile doch . . . Oh stay, thou are so beautiful." Here he accepts what, according to the present argument, had become the characteristic behavior of his imagination.

6

Small wonder, then, that some of the poems of this spring season should be so short and so inchoate. Nature is inseparable from happiness, and increasingly indistinguishable from the light by which one sees and which, after all, is also *what* one sees. The image, in which one's happiness translates itself, is no more durable than the condition of the light. It is transient at best, and yet it is the entire object of poetry.

Such considerations prompt an attempt to obtain a rereading of "O saisons, ô châteaux" on the grounds that such obscure poems are sometimes easier to come to grips with if the reader is fully aware of the reasons for their obscurity.

O saisons, ô châteaux,
Quelle âme est sans défauts?

O saisons, ô châteaux,

J'ai fait la magique étude
Du Bonheur, que nul n'élude.

O vive lui, chaque fois
Que chante le coq gaulois.

Mais! je n'aurai plus d'envie,
Il s'est chargé de ma vie,

Ce Charme! il prit âme et corps,
Et dispersa tous efforts.

Que comprendre à ma parole?
Il fait qu'elle fuie et vole!

O saisons, ô châteaux.

[Et, si le malheur m'entraîne,
Sa disgrâce m'est certaine.

Il faut que son dédain, las!
Me livre au plus prompt trépas!

– O Saisons, ô châteaux!]

From a first inspection it is at least certain that this is not the kind of obscurity that challenges the readers of Valéry and Mallarmé. It does not arise from a technique of hiding the first terms of metaphors. Mallarmé's swan, Valéry's "tranquil roof," are to be understood as representing something else than a bird and a part of a house. But these "saisons" are seasons, these "châteaux" are châteaux. Rimbaud is not constructing a rebus, a puzzle to be solved.

But it is helpful, even so, to compare Rimbaud and Valéry at one point: Valéry, like Rimbaud, is dealing with a landscape. He reveals it gradually in the poem, and the act of revelation has a great deal to do, we suspect, with the pleasure the poet takes in his creation.

A large measure of Rimbaud's obscurity is similar in that it comes from the involvement of his poems in a landscape, but different from Valéry's in that he invariably fails to reveal the landscape's organization. He *refers* to features in the landscape which his imagination sees, as if the reader knew already what they were and their relation to each other. Hence his specifying use of the definite article and of the demonstrative pronoun:

> Zut alors, si le soleil quitte *ces* bords . . .
> Que pouvais-je boire dans *cette* jeune Oise . . .
> Sous *les* bosquets l'aube évapore . . .
> *L'*eau claire; comme le sel des larmes d'enfance . . .
>
> (Italics mine.)

They limit and identify: we are here, by this water or looking at these woods—and not elsewhere. There will be no gradual fuller revelation, just as there will be no rebus. A considerable part of Rimbaud's obscurity comes, in other words, from his not telling the reader what the reader needs to know. In poems earlier than 1872, this tendency of Rimbaud's to say little about the scene itself is already remarkable; now it has become characteristic; it will remain so through the prose *Illuminations*.

Yet though we never see the poet's landscape completely, we do become familiar after a while with its component parts. There are generally trees, and he often tells us their names; there are expanses of briar, and fields with flowers in them, and stretches of grass. Water is frequently present: rivers, streams, ponds, and moats. In all this nature there is repeated reference to structure in stone: the streamside parapet which becomes a rampart in "Mémoire," an "old court of honor" in "Michel et Christine," a "highest tower" in, naturally, "La Chanson de la plus haute tour," a "château mouillé" in "Comédie de la soif," and in "Age d'Or" for no reason visibly connected with the economy of the poem as a whole, there is an unexpected—but now highly suggestive—exclamation: "O joli château!"

From what has been said above about the relation of felicity to nature, to light, and eventually to weather, and from the recognition of the elements which keep turning up in Rimbaud's internal landscape, the thrice repeated cry, "O saisons, ô châteaux," becomes intelligible. Seasons are weather, and châteaux are a prominent, perhaps dominant, feature of the landscape his imagination has dwelt upon. They have been the focus of his poetic activity, of his search for felicity.

The search has not always succeeded, and success, when achieved at all, has been transient. As he had foreseen as early as the "Lettre du voyant," and as we gather from poems written even earlier that he was disposed to believe, the poetic enterprise requires a strong soul, perhaps one much stronger than his. Thus failures have been inevitable: "Quelle âme est sans défauts?" But the "magic study" has been carried out. This is every man's study to make, at least to the extent that no one knows what "wood will awaken to find itself a violin." And it is "magic," not necessarily because Rimbaud had been in contact, as has been suggested, with the "white" magic of esoteric cults or because he is familiar with the rituals of alchemy; from observing Rimbaud in those instances when he has obviously been happy one has a reasonably clear idea of what happiness meant to him and, accordingly, we have every license to believe that by magic he means the prescription outlined in the "Lettre du voyant." And if this is the case, the next two couplets may be taken to repeat what he has said elsewhere also—to be precise, in the "Bateau ivre."

Whatever the meaning of "le coq gaulois"—and a sexual one is not automatically excluded—his felicity clearly takes the form of a delight for which, in turn, he pays by a kind of paralysis. Impotence follows bliss, and so does helplessness. (This would be a defect of the soul grievous enough to justify the second line of the first couplet.) Its final effect is to make his poetry obscure and elusive:

> Que comprendre à ma parole?
> Il fait qu'elle fuie et vole.

Thus, "O saisons, ô châteaux" can be read as a brief account of a poet's development. It may thus be significant that it finishes as it begins, with a salute to the materials of his occupation. A poem of reconciliation with one's destiny does not have to be a shout of triumph. It is perhaps enough to expect of his poetic process that once in a while it bring him a sort of beatitude even if, at other times, it should fail wretchedly to do so. He recognizes his limitations and, for this moment at least, is willing to take them — and himself — as they are. It is true that such poems, in which he does not cry out in frustration or defeat, are rare in Rimbaud's work. More often he ends suspended between the two flowers he cannot reach.

7

The acceptance can have been only momentary. The bulk of the evidence indicates that he was very aware of his failure, before he even began, so far as we know, the *Illuminations*. Those who can accept the notion that he was an *Eidetiker* would of course have an explanation ready-made for the collapse of his enterprise: as the subject leaves adolescence behind, the brightness of the eidetic images normally fades, and they may disappear altogether. But the obvious objection here would be hard to overcome: there is no lack of brilliance in the images either of these last poems or of the *Illuminations*. What they lack is durability and, more and more, organization.

The process of giving over verse in favor of poetic prose had begun, not only in the general slackening of his interest in verse, which may after all have been involuntary, but also in an actual change in practice which we know about even though the manuscript in question remains lost. This was the poem in prose to which Verlaine, long after the event and when he could no longer put his hands on the papers, gave the title of "La Chasse spirituelle." Just what this piece was is conjectural. Verlaine obviously admired it, but his references are guarded and include no specific description. If it was the packet that Verlaine's estranged wife destroyed under the impression that it contained a correspondence which might one day embarrass her son, we may suspect that the contents formed some sort of epithalamium celebrating the homosexual relationship. And, to be mistaken for a letter or letters, the manuscript had to be in prose. But the whole story is tantalizingly vague. Mathilde Verlaine was probably truthful, but certainly unsophisticated about literature; Paul Verlaine remembered the piece when he was summoning up a past which had been abundantly preserved in alcohol. For present purposes, it is merely evidence that Rimbaud had already turned away from verse.

Had he discovered that the material of his fugitive visions was ill-suited to treatment in the regular, consecrated rhythms? This does not rule out, of course, the possibility that it was also becoming more elusive. "If what he [the poet] brings back from Out There," he had written Demeny, "is formed, he will give it form; if it is unformed, he will leave it formless." We may interpret the remark to suit our purpose: poetic form, rhythm, rhyme, is order and organization. These imply a certain permanence in the material treated. One can imagine a material so volatile and elusive that any attempt to regiment it in verse would come to seem like nothing less than falsification.

Prose, like that of the *Illuminations,* could represent a possibility of superior faithfulness.

Chapter VIII — The New Language

A READER whose native language is English must revise some fundamental notions about poetry when he approaches the *Illuminations.** We do not even have a convenient English term for what the French call *poème en prose,* probably because we have never felt a real need for one. Our poets have not had to work in a verse tradition which emphasizes subtle variation within a superficial monotony. The stress system of English permits, as French verse does not, rhythm separated from rhyme. And not being traditionally familiar with the "tyranny of verse," we are unlikely to understand to what ex-

* He will be well advised to provide himself with the excellent translations, by Louise Varese, of both the *Illuminations* (Norfolk, Conn.: New Directions, 1946) and *Une Saison en enfer* (1945).

tent the adoption of the poem in prose could constitute the unfettering of a French poet.

Any author of a prose poem has given up verse but not poetry, and the primary qualities of his vehicle are poetic ones: rich suggestiveness, condensation, multiplication of meanings, and occasional paradox. He is likely to feel, also, that abandoning verse makes possible a greater "purity," a poetic statement less contaminated by unpoetic elements, more immediately expressive. No doubt there was still another advantage for Rimbaud. The radical discontinuity which the medium permits makes it an excellent instrument for following the contours of broken and chaotic visions. If his visions had no form, as he said in the "Lettre du voyant," he would bring back non-form. But it would be a mistake to overemphasize this one motive among the several possible ones. Not all of the *Illuminations* report ecstatic visions; the variety of their substance is broad. (How broad we may postpone saying until the place is reached to take an inventory.) It is enough to point out that the flexibility of a prose which is not so much a prose in the discursive sense as it is a non-verse, would have advantages for dealing with an imagery which we know to have been unstable.

The prose of the *Illuminations* is both an extraordinary medium and one which the poet adopted in full awareness of what he was doing. Poems like "Antique," his brief and shining evocation of Pan, show that he was perfectly able to write a communicative and continuous prose when he pleased; the truth must be that more often than not he did not please to do so, preferring a highly personal syntax and a private vocabulary. He had said in the "Lettre du voyant" that the poet would have to use a new language.

Like any language, it may be learned.

"Matinée d'ivresse" makes a good starting point because it

associates examples of syntax and vocabulary with a subject which is already familiar:

> O *mon* Bien! O *mon* Beau! Fanfare atroce où je ne trébuche point! Chevalet féerique! Hourra pour l'œuvre inouïe et pour le corps merveilleux, pour la première fois! Cela commença sous les rires des enfants, cela finira par eux. Ce poison va rester dans toutes nos veines même quand, la fanfare tournant, nous serons rendus à l'ancienne inharmonie. O maintenant, nous si digne de ces tortures! rassemblons fervemment cette promesse surhumaine faite à notre corps et à notre âme créés: cette promesse, cette démence! L'élégance, la science, la violence! On nous a promis d'enterrer dans l'ombre l'arbre du bien et du mal, de déporter les honnêtetés tyranniques, afin que nous amenions notre très pur amour. Cela commença par quelques dégoûts et cela finit, — ne pouvant nous saisir sur-le-champ de cette éternité, — cela finit par une débandade de parfums.
>
> Rire des enfants, discrétion des esclaves, austérité des vierges, horreur des figures et des objets d'ici, sacrés soyez-vous par le souvenir de cette veille. Cela commençait par toute la rustrerie, voici que cela finit par des anges de flamme et de glace.
>
> Petite veille d'ivresse, sainte! quand ce ne serait que pour le masque dont tu nous as gratifié. Nous t'affirmons, méthode! Nous n'oublions pas que tu as glorifié hier chacun de nos âges. Nous avons foi au poison. Nous savons donner notre vie tout entière tous les jours.
>
> Voici le temps des *Assassins*.

We gather that he has somehow experienced or contemplated the good and the beautiful, and the capitals suggest that these are supreme of their kind; the title makes us assume the use of an intoxicant. But in what way are the good and beautiful so specially his? Does the emphasis on the possessives mean that they are his and his alone, or simply that, after long desire, he has at last attained the experience of them and thus, so to speak, entered upon possession? The "première fois," just below, may influence us toward the second reading; if so, a question immediately rises as to how early in the development of his great experiment this piece was written. And just what was the experience?

"Fanfare atroce" links an idea of music with one of frightfulness, and the statement that he did not stumble is reminiscent of his apprehension in the "Lettre du voyant" lest he "fall back" at the crucial moment. "Chevalet" having among its meanings the designation of a kind of torture rack, one recalls his earlier statement to Izambard that the sufferings were "atrocious," and the association of this with "féerique" can be taken to affirm that through them he has been admitted to realms which are not ours. Thus the hurrah of success—a success which is the unheard of achievement: we take it that he has seen what he called in the "Lettre du voyant" that which other men have only glimpsed.

Now, at last, we get a sentence having a principal verb—in fact, two principal verbs—but again his syntax balks us: the reference of "cela" is not clear; we have to assume that it means the whole experience—and we still do not know what the experience was. (His procedure recalls the landscapes of the verse poems of 1872, in which he knows so much better than we what he is talking about.) The laughter of the children brings an additional problem: the meaning could be that in an early stage of the working of the intoxicant he heard the sweet sounds, but his use of the preposition "sous" could carry the suggestion that the laughter was hostile—why? (If, incidentally, this laughter is transformed, as the dream intensifies, into the fanfare, we have here an example of the metamorphosis of an image which is not, as in earlier work, visual, but auditory.)

The next sentence, again grammatically complete and this time not so puzzling, affirms that something will remain after the fanfare has moved away. We know at least that the "former absence of harmony" is opposed to the present fanfare—which, accordingly, must be a harmony; and we are sure now that the music of the dream was indeed a delight as well as frightening. But language fails him; just what the ecstasy was is too much, if not for words, at least for sentences; he can only exclaim.

Above, he has linked the "œuvre inouïe" with a "marvelous body"—his own, or, as in "Being beauteous," one of which he has a vision? At that juncture it is impossible for us to know. But now, following the cry about being worthy of these tortures, we learn of the promise made "to our created body and soul," and suspect that he has felt himself to be transfigured. The enumeration of abstractions which follows conveys at most the feelings which characterize the ecstasy. They still do not describe it. But we do learn, following this, that the promise had been to "bury the tree of good and evil," to go beyond the tyranny of decency, to the attainment of "supremely pure love."

Here we notice that beginning with "Ce poison" the original singular possessive has been replaced by the plural. Who shares in the "our"? More than one person has participated in the ecstasy, and if the other one is Verlaine, then we know what kind of love this was. (Even "pure" is ambiguous, since it may mean either "blameless" or "unadulterated.")

Does the next "cela" refer to the opening stages of his intoxication, or to the "pure love"? In any case, one gathers that the state of beatitude was transitory—as usual—and that, as he relives the experience, it is drawing to a close. "Cela finira" above, has given way to "cela finit"; the present has replaced the future. And in the final paragraph, exactly as in the "Bateau ivre," all is retrospective.

We learn now that, as we would naturally have suspected, the "method" of the "Lettre du voyant," has proved itself. And the famous "Voici le temps des *Assassins*" may be taken as an indirect reference, since the members of the old assassin associations of thugee were hashish smokers, to the particular type of intoxicant which has produced the vision.

Obviously, Rimbaud abandons normal syntax just where the reader will be sure to miss it most, leaving him with the hope that he has understood at least in part, and with the absolute knowledge that he has not understood completely. "Matinée d'ivresse" is not entirely hermetic, but the faithful reader of the *Illuminations* returns to it repeatedly precisely because despite his best efforts there remains some element of enigma.

Rimbaud's habitual procedure is to use a substantive in a situation where there would normally be an entire sentence, or, conversely, to exploit sentences which function only as complex substantives. Examples are numerous everywhere in these texts. For instance, the beginning of "Parades": "Des drôles très solides." The "drôles" simply exist, in the vision, as if stripped of all relationships: we are not told what, when, how, why, or where. They are *because* they are. "Les Ponts" begins: "Des ciels gris de crystal." The third division of "Enfances" consists of an anaphora which repeats the statement "il y a" and affirms in sequence the unqualified, unconditioned existence of a bird, a clock, a lair of an animal, a cathedral, and a child's carriage. Why objects are enumerated in one order rather than another, and what relationships there may be between them, the reader is left to guess. No style could be more extremely elliptical, and much of the effort of interpreting such texts must go into finding plausible substitutions for the ellipses.

Thus it has to be the reader who creates the coherence implied in any interpretation. In the instance of "Enfances," we have the evidence of the poem as a whole that the poet is calling up scenes from his very early life to contrast with his present state, and assume that here he is speaking in the voice and manner of a child young enough, actually, not to make connections between objects. In addition, one small detail which may serve to guide the reader is hidden in the part which contains the elliptical anaphora just quoted: that is, the uncertainty as to whether the child's carriage has been abandoned in the bushes or whether it has rolled off alone down the slope. The uncertainty, explicitly stated in the poem, is enough to suggest that the image is not entirely clear to the poet himself, and that the evocation has not succeeded. Our feeling that his efforts may be only partly successful may in turn encourage us to feel that the order in which images appear in such a passage as this could be determined by the ease or difficulty with which they respond to the call and consequently take the place of the context and tone which in ordinary prose makes us distribute emphasis as the author intends. Thus the responsibility for the emphases becomes ours. Each one provides an opportunity to misread.

There are numerous such pitfalls in the jungle of Rimbaud's syntax. Not only are the sentences so often nominal and indistinguishable in function from complex substantives, but main verbs are frequently omitted altogether. "Barbare," for example, does not use a single one. Or else the verb usurps the role of an adjective; in a phrase like "Des oiseaux comédiens s'abattent sur un ponton de maçonnerie" ("Scènes"), the fact of the birds' alighting is in effect part of the image of the birds and could be handled by a relative clause or a participle; except for the *force* of the image, nothing would be changed. And just as characteristically, those parts of speech which fix the relationships of subordination and coordination, sequence, equivalence, cause and effect, are frequently absent. Pronouns, especially the demonstratives, are used with the vaguest of references; "cela," in "Matinée d'ivresse," is typical. Clearly, Rimbaud resisted the restraints of syntax as much as those of verse.

The reference in the text to "notre très pur amour" serves notice that the main questions as to vocabulary will continue to cluster around Rimbaud's eternal themes of love, nature, and freedom. As it happens, nature is absent from this particular text; freedom, on the other hand, is in evidence — but the notion has expanded considerably since the time when being free consisted of getting away from Vitalie Rimbaud. The "promise" — a word which itself needs explaining, since it may refer either to the program of the "Lettre du voyant" or to something Rimbaud had read — had included freedom from the "tree of good and evil" and the restrictions of ordinary middle class morality; one might almost say, from Church and family. It has been realized, apparently, and now, as formerly, freedom is freedom to love.

But "amour" here is another ambiguous term. We shall find it used elsewhere in the *Illuminations* in at least three different possible meanings. One of these we shall find — surprisingly perhaps — to be an ordinary, normal love of women; another will be a part of Rimbaud's transcendental politics, his dream of a world where all men shall love and be inherently decent toward each other; the third, of course, would be his affair with Verlaine.

There is a good chance that the third possibility is the strongest. The testimony of Bouillane de Lacoste's critical edition notwithstanding, this text would seem one of the earlier among the *Illuminations*. The references in it to the program of voyancy, and to the taking of a narcotic, sound very much as if it dated from the time of active experimentation, and certainly from before a moment when he could have written the text called "Vagabonds," after his warmth toward his "pitiable brother" had been largely replaced by scorn. This appears to have been the moment when their homosexual relationship came nearest meriting to be called love. We may not be absolutely sure, since

"Honte," with its evidence that the course of their affair was not always smooth, also dates from the spring of 1872—and one would not look for an *Illumination* in prose to have been written much earlier. That the word refers to their homosexuality is only the most plausible reading.

There are words like "fanfare" in this text which will turn out to belong to the clusters which form around these three themes of Rimbaud's. But it is of course impossible to come to recognize these from the study of one text alone, and our investigation of the vocabulary—though not of the syntax, which will remain what we have seen it to be—must be pursued through the remaining *Illuminations.*

2

In the preceding text, liberty and love were associated, but not nature. In "Aube," on the other hand, nature and love are assimilated with each other, while liberty remains outside the picture.

J'ai embrassé l'aube d'été.

Rien ne bougeait encore au front des palais. L'eau était morte. Les camps d'ombres ne quittaient pas la route du bois. J'ai marché, réveillant les haleines vives et tièdes, et les pierreries regardèrent, et les ailes se levèrent sans bruit.

La première entreprise fut, dans le sentier déjà empli de frais et blêmes éclats, une fleur qui me dit son nom.

Je ris au wasserfall blond qui s'échevela à travers les sapins: à la cime argentée je reconnus la déesse.

Alors je levai un à un les voiles. Dans l'allée, en agitant les bras. Par la plaine, où je l'ai dénoncée au coq. A la grand'ville elle fuyait parmi les clochers et les dômes, et courant comme un mendiant sur les quais de marbre, je la chassais.

En haut de la route, près d'un bois de lauriers, je l'ai entourée avec ses voiles amassés, et j'ai senti un peu son immense corps. L'aube et l'enfant tombèrent au bas du bois.

Au réveil il était midi.

Surely there is no need of insisting that this is a poem of euphoria, or that its author is the Rimbaud who has long been familiar. The speaker has seen, pursued, and, although he refers to himself as a "child," lain with the Dawn. Qualified critics have considered that the account includes orgasm. The elements of the formula are as old as "Sensation"—he has been with nature and has been happy "as if with a woman."

Significantly for our purpose, this nature poem, which has been called one of the world's greatest, is entirely without natural description. Elements of a landscape are present, but no landscape. Everything is treated referentially: there must be a body of water, because we are told that the water is "dead"; there has to be a wood, since he lies in the shadow of one; because he sees the disheveled blondness of the waterfall through the trees, and a flower tells him its name, there must be a waterfall and a flower.

One recognizes his familiar habit. In the poems of spring, 1872, he was referring repeatedly to a landscape which he did not describe. But he did refer, then, to objective elements in the landscape, whereas here his attention goes first not to the objects but to their effect on him; for example, it goes first to the disheveled blondness, and only afterward to the waterfall. Coupled with the tendency he has shown ever since "Le Dormeur du val," to see refractions of light rather than the objects which refract them, such a habit of vision disintegrates nature.

We get half-caught glimpses, sometimes very beautiful—a few flowers in the wind, some yards of talus, a stretch of lawn—which the reader is not able to organize in a picture and which are not organized for him by the poet. Sometimes, also, the animal and vegetable realms blend with the metallic and mineral. In "Aube," precious stones look at the poet, and a flower talks; in "Fleurs," stones and metals are associated to an extent such that a flower seen in a jeweled setting almost becomes a jewel among the others; a glitter of sunlight falls upon silks, gauzes, velvet, and crystal, all of which, like bronze, become black in the sunlight; pieces of gold strewn on agate, pillars of mahogany supporting a dome of emeralds, bouquets of white satin, and delicate shafts of rubies all but obscure the water lily they surround. The principal effect is one of dazzlement so great that objects exchange identities.

In "Marine," the replacement of nature by a play of light is the making of the whole poem. The central metaphor is as banal as possible: everyone has at some time equated the prow of a ship with a plough. The interest of the poem comes from its bringing such a metaphor back to life. Plough and ship first appear as being metal "cars"; the prow which beats through the water in one line becomes the share uprooting briars in the next; currents flow through the earth and the sea's surface is furrowed—and these marks recede toward what may be equally well distant treetops or the high places along a jetty.

Les chars d'argent et de cuivre—
Les proues d'acier et d'argent—
Battent l'écume,—
Soulèvent les souches des ronces.
Les courants de la lande,
Et les ornières immenses du reflux,
Filent circulairement vers l'est,
Vers les piliers de la forêt,—
Vers les fûts de la jetée,
Dont l'angle est heurté par des tourbillons de lumière.

Here the metaphor creates a fusion: two sets of phenomena

are so identified that we hardly know which we are looking at; it is impossible to say which term of the metaphor is "tenor" and which is "vehicle." For present purposes it is important that the metaphorical identity, our inability to distinguish plough from prow, is revealed or established by a "tourbillon" of light. Just what such a whirlwind of light could be remains the poet's secret, but the word obviously records a highly private and subjective response to the particular light condition. But in view of the changes brought about by a shift in lighting in "Larme," "Mémoire," and "Michel et Christine," "Marine" should be read as if it consisted of two principal statements, one of the identity expressed in the metaphor, and the other of the unusualness of an illumination which not only does not alter or dissipate under contemplation but also makes the metaphor itself possible. "Marine" need not be called a great poem; there is only one flash, one insight—and not into the nature of things in general but merely of two specific things. But the certain slant of light has conducted the poet to an epiphany, though a minor one. And light, here, is nature. When Rimbaud wrote that the light of certain skies had refined his vision—"Certains ciels ont raffiné mon optique"—he was telling a literal truth.

He may by this time have been only infrequently capable of imagining a coherent picture, but his capacity for *feeling* nature, as opposed to *seeing*, appears to have remained intact. In "Après le déluge" the feeling of supernal freshness after rain is reminiscent of the epidermal response first recorded in "Sensation"—and the feeling is an essential part of the poem's meaning. In "Aube" the feeling of the goodness of nature in the first light of morning is solid and unbroken. Other examples would include "Ornières" and "Enfance."

In brief, Rimbaud remains the poet of nature he has been before, but in the language he uses now oblique references either to an infinitesimal fragment of a scene, to its effect on his eye, or to his response replace the explicit and overt.

3

While nature thus acquires a remarkably extensive set of implications and overtones in the *Illuminations,* love acquires even more. Once, his euphorias had induced in him a desire to reach out beyond the ego, so vague that he could then identify it only as erotic. ("Heureux comme avec une femme.") By the time of the *Illuminations* the impulse becomes at once more various and, in its different manifestations, more sharply defined.

Even now, of course, the familiar phantasy of "Premier baiser" and "Les Réparties de Nina" does not entirely disappear. Despite the renunciation of the love of women recorded in "Mes petites amoureuses" and "Les Sœurs de charité," which may in any case have had the complete gratuity of giving up what he had never possessed, a surprising number of female figures appear in the prose poems and, again surprisingly, in ways which suggest a normal sexuality. Rimbaud's ecstasies sometimes take the form of physical enjoyment, as in "Aube." There is a queen, as well as a king, in "Royauté." "Phrases" refers to "*ma* camarade, mendiante, enfant monstre." A couple—the girl wears a gingham skirt—figures in "Ouvriers." In "Bottom" the speaker flees in shame, because of his own inadequacy, from his mistress and her "chefs-d'œuvre physiques." He has met, he says in "Vies," all the women of the old painters. A series of four women is invoked in "Dévotion."

Temptations to rewrite Rimbaud's biography because of this persistence of the female in his poems are to be resisted: arguments that he was not homosexual founder under the weight of common sense. The evidence of the writings is flimsy support for Izambard's contention that the poet's departures from the norm were experimental and tentative. The *Illuminations* called "H" and "Vagabonds" quite counteract it. We can only say that whatever his life was like, it is true that in his visions of bliss women outnumber men.

These visions are abundantly erotic. Dawn, in "Aube," is little else. At the end of "Phrases" there is an explicit statement about attaining erotic euphoria: "I lower the lamp, throw myself on my bed, and, turning toward the side where the shadow is, I see you, my girls! my queens!" Because of the ambiguity of the French, "filles" may mean his daughters here, that is, his creations; if so, they would be no less erotic, and no less present. In the allegory called "Conte," there even appears a curious line in which the women the Prince slaughters refuse to remain dead, and one may wonder, remembering Rimbaud's own ritual slaughter of love partners during the winter of 1870–1871 ("Mes petites amoureuses"), whether this later text does not report, guardedly, that it is one thing to put women out of the imagination, but another to make them stay out.

For our purpose the matter is of no moment except in so far as it continues to identify euphoria with the erotic. Much more relevant would be to know whether the erotic was a precondition of physical felicity for Rimbaud, or whether, the other way round, one of his ways of saying that he felt good was to say that he experienced the stirrings of sex. In the *Illuminations* and elsewhere, erotic expression may be a kind of shorthand for recording emotions not specifically erotic at all. If so, we must add that this habit of notation is a very persistent one.

The *Illuminations* also speak repeatedly of "the new love," and, most relevantly to what interests the present study, only in poems that are about euphoria or in those in which Rimbaud speaks of his "method." Whether this is exactly the same as his "very pure" love is a matter of conjecture — as is also the question in given cases of whether he means love for Verlaine or a vaguely effusive, semipolitical or utopian love for the human race. What is certain is that the expression so often occurs in conjunction with references to music or to strength ("force," "énergie"), that all three terms become synonyms in the language of euphoria.

Previously, music has occupied Rimbaud's attention infrequently if at all. Now it is everywhere. There is "musique savante" in "Conte"; "musique rauque" clashes with "musique sourde" in "Being beauteous," and the harsh music drives away the muted; the poet is represented as a musician in "Vies"; there are further references to music in "Matinée d'ivresse," "Les Ponts," the first of the two "Villes," "Vagabonds," "Métropolitain," "Barbare," "Promontoire," "Soir historique," and "Solde." Furthermore, this is no ordinary music: in "A une raison" it is called a "new harmony," and in "Soir historique" it is obviously something never heard by other men; elsewhere it consists of "mélodies impossibles," of singing "the lives of peoples," or of a shimmering visual effect like that of rising heat.

However awkward the term "felt music" must be, it is clearly the best one for what Rimbaud is talking about. The experience of it is notably synaesthetic. Several passages offer convincing evidence that by "harmonie" he meant something very like what Baudelaire meant by order—but an order *audible* to the imagination—a transcendent feeling of the rightness of everything. He identifies a "musical house" with a state of complete fellow feeling in "Phrases"; when the fanfare in "Matinée d'ivresse" retires a former disharmony returns; a touch of a finger to a drum brings a "new Harmony" into being in "A une raison." There are thus times when it seems that by music he meant not the thing itself but an internal disposition such as one might experience when certain music was played.

Accordingly, when he declares, in "Vies," not only that he

is an inventor more worthy than his predecessors but he is "even a musician who has found something lik to love," we know what he means. The claim is pe telligible in the light of the "Lettre du voyant." It is stronger claim when left in French than it seems in translation, for in French it involves a pun: he has found the *clef* in which love may be "played." Thus music and the affective state which he calls "new love" are affirmed to be identical; and from all this it emerges that music is attached to an internal state which he seeks not to describe so much as to express, to which are attached also new love, harmony, health, strength, energy. Their relation to each other is inescapable. "O palmes! diamant—Amour! force!" he cries in "Angoisse." In "Solde," he speaks of "l'éveil fraternel de toutes les énergies chorales et orchestrales." In "Génie," he joins "l'affection et l'avenir, la force et l'amour."

Like his syntax, Rimbaud's vocabulary is so private that at times it seems to have been invented *ad hoc*. One comes finally to the conclusion that both were born of a desperate need to express in its totality a unique disposition of the psyche. In this, of course, Rimbaud was following the characteristic development of modern European literature—if indeed he was not breaking trail—in its headlong rush toward complete subjectivism. Feeling—unique, personal, perhaps idiosyncratic feeling—is all, not in Goethe's sense alone, but also in that of a generation which will innovate even to the extent of placing the focus of narration, in its novels, within the psyche of a chosen character.

Chapter IX – The New Poetry

THE ILLUMINATIONS must be approached in the humility of ignorance. We do not even know that Rimbaud intended these texts to form a single aesthetic whole: his having copied out the first twenty-six in the order in which we now read them may indicate some such intention, but we know what this order was only because he copied more than one to the page, and it could just as easily be that he merely wanted fair copies and could afford to use only the minimum amount of paper. And there are fifteen additional texts which he did not copy, leaving the reader to his own devices.

Even the assumption that Rimbaud considered all the texts as we have them to be finished work is precisely that – an assumption. The chance that some of them, at least, are sketches for poems not subsequently completed may not be entirely dismissed. It makes us wary to realize that in the "Alchimie du verbe" chapter of *Une Saison en enfer,* the poems he scatters through the pages in which he deplores the excesses of his great venture — as if inviting the reader to share his disgust — are not the prose texts but verse. In brief, our notion of what the *Illuminations* are, of the legitimacy of treating them as a group, of when they were written, and of why they were written in prose, is formed from a mixture of internal evidence and more or less enlightened guess work.

It would be of some help to know what the title means. Verlaine's report, that Rimbaud had in mind the English "painted plates," is hardly more suggestive than the common idea that the reference is to the embellishment of old manuscripts. Such possibilities have no more to support them than the less recondite one that an illumination is, after all, a flash, and that one of the French words for persons who are vouchsafed occasional moments of deep perception is "illuminé." My own persistence in using "epiphany" and "moments privilégiés," like my commitment to the theory that the search for escape through epiphany was the subject of the "Lettre du voyant," implies my subscription to reading "illumination" to mean flash. Doing so makes some of the texts more intelligible.

Some — but by no means all. For these pieces are not all of the same sort of poetic utterance, and thus are not susceptible to being opened by the same "key." Some nine, according to my count, bear directly upon the subject of felicity, and so would justify my understanding of the title. So would the additional number which reverse the medal and are about the absence of felicity. Others, like "Solde," might be included under the same rubric because they treat the poetic process which was supposed to bring him bliss. But the total of these is smaller than the total number of the *Illuminations.*

From a slightly different point of view the variation, even between pieces within these groups, is wide indeed. "Aube," "Matinée d'ivresse," "Being beauteous," "Marine," and "Barbare," all involve—if I am right—the experience of euphoria through what may be called an epiphany. But "Matinée d'ivresse," as already noted, deals mainly with the process of attaining the vision, whereas the other four attempt to deal with the vision itself: "Aube" is a visionary experience of nature and we have seen "Marine" to be a piece of perfect metaphoric perception, while "Being beauteous" is about a vision in metamorphosis, and "Barbare" about a series of hallucinations associated with one euphoric state. Some of the texts cannot but be autobiographical: "Vagabonds," for example, could easily have found a place in the "Epoux infernal" section of *Une Saison en enfer*; "Ville," and "Angoisse," have to do with a desperate personal situation such as Rimbaud's toward the beginning of *Une Saison*; "Jeunesse" and "Vies" trace the stages of a career, and "Solde" appears to be an attempt to sum one up. On the other hand, "Royauté" and "Conte" are allegorical tales; texts like "Villes" are paintings of city scenes; "Génie," as I understand it, is the poet's examination of his own personality; "H" is about either masturbation or sexual heterodoxy. And there are still others which defy attempts at brief statement of their nature.

In view of such variety, as well as of the ignorance we are condemned to work in, it is preferable to study the *Illuminations* as a collection of separate, discrete poems in which the same themes frequently recur but which cannot be demonstrated to have a common subject or an "architecture." They do share an unusual intensity and a kind of purity which arise no more from their matter than from the condensation possible by virtue of their being in prose, of the reader's not being distracted by the apparatus of regular rhythm and rhyme, and of the prevalence of ellipsis. The same qualities are often the cause of the reader's bafflement, also.

Even if he had not been warned in the introduction, the reader of these chapters would have discovered that they cannot pretend to any completeness of interpretation. Here, as before, they are not meant to relieve the reader of effort, but to suggest possible attitudes and dispositions toward the material, and to direct his attention. As before, the major focus will be on what, in another poet, might be called recurrent themes.

2

One appears in the first of the texts, "Après le déluge";

Aussitôt que l'idée du Déluge se fut rassise, Un lièvre s'arrêta dans les sainfoins et les clochettes mouvantes et dit sa prière à l'arc-en-ciel à travers la toile de l'araignée.

Oh! les pierres précieuses qui se cachaient, — les fleurs qui regardaient déjà.

Dans la grande rue sale les étals se dressèrent, et l'on tira les barques vers la mer étagée là-haut comme sur les gravures.

Le sang coula, chez Barbe-Bleue, — aux abattoirs, — dans les cirques, où le sceau de Dieu blêmit les fenêtres. Le sang et le lait coulèrent.

Les castors bâtirent. Les "mazagrans" fumèrent dans les estaminets.

Dans la grande maison de vitres encore ruisselante les enfants en deuil regardèrent les merveilleuses images.

Une porte claqua, — et sur la place du hameau, l'enfant tourna ses bras, compris des girouettes et des coqs des clochers de partout, sous l'éclatante giboulée.

Madame * * * établit un piano dans les Alpes. La messe et les premières communions se célébrèrent aux cent mille autels de la cathédrale.

Les caravanes partirent. Et le Splendide-Hôtel fut bâti dans le chaos de glaces et de nuit du pôle.

Depuis lors, la Lune entendit les chacals piaulant par les déserts de thym, — et les églogues en sabots grognant dans le verger. Puis, dans la futaie violette, bourgeonnante, Eucharis me dit que c'était le printemps.

Sourds, étang, — Écume, roule sur le pont et pardessus les bois; — draps noirs et orgues, — éclairs et tonnerre, — montez et roulez; — Eaux et tristesses, montez et relevez les Déluges.

Car depuis qu'ils se sont dissipés, — oh les pierres précieuses s'enfouissant, et les fleurs ouvertes! — c'est un ennui! et la Reine, la Sorcière qui allume sa braise dans le pot de terre, ne voudra jamais nous raconter ce qu'elle sait, et que nous ignorons.

At the beginning the world is good, fresh, moist, clean. The Deluge — any rainstorm recalls the biblical flood — has purified and made everything primitively lovely. But commerce, industry, and civilization establish themselves: there are images of darkness and blood. What is needed is another flood, to bring about another purification.

And the fresh world is a child's world: the point of view at the beginning is set at the height of a hare. Through rain-washed windows children may look at wonderful books. The little boy, waving his arms in the village square while the rain still falls, recalls the other boy, in "Aube," who waves his arms as he pursues Dawn. This world of childhood is one where everything is alive: stones hide themselves, flowers watch you and speak their names (again as in "Aube"). And this is the world which is subsequently destroyed.

In other words, new symbols have replaced the cool, dark woman of the river bed in "Mémoire," but the burden is the same: a time of childhood and innocence was very good, but it has passed. No matter how much of this text mystifies us — myriad attempts have been made to explain, or explain away, the lady with her piano in the Alps — the central theme stands out as we shall also find it to stand out at the beginning of *Une Saison en enfer*.

This, we note, constitutes a commentary on the nature of felicity: it is infinitely more attainable in youth, disappears with age — or at least becomes more difficult of attainment. Characteristically, also, the poem flays what frustrates the delight of the soul, and the images of the invocation, "Sourds, étang . . . ," have some of the destructiveness and violence critics have found in much of the later work.

"Enfance," the second text, and "Vies," both of which sound autobiographical, repeat the same formula. Beginning with the scene in which nature shines resplendently and with the hint that the time of day when people have to be in the house is an enormous bore, "Enfance" moves into a second section which seems a reminiscence of a small girl's funeral — with the corpse being brought down the doorstep, a creaking of wheels on sand, a scene in a cemetery — and then into a whole series of images of emptiness. The third section is a naming ritual, with a child's voice stating the existence of a series of objects; the fourth identifies him as now advanced in age, with images of a saint in prayer, a savant at work, a pedestrian on the road. The poem closes with the speaker ready for a tomb and feeling trapped underground in some unpleasant city.

"Vies" also attaches images of pleasure to a former moment. There are memories of silver and sunny hours when the hand of a companion is on his shoulder and there are caresses. These are opposed to a present in which he inhabits a bitter country and is an exile from the earlier scene; experience has worn life out; he is eaten by skepticism and perhaps on the way to becoming "a very dangerous madman."

This, we may repeat, is a commentary on happiness. It is not one in which the necessity for being young replaces any of the familiar ingredients in the formula. It would be more correct to say that wherever we find the theme in the *Illuminations* it qualifies the others, without displacing them: childhood is the time when one is happy *in* nature; with the years one is deprived of nature, and is correspondingly deprived of felicity. In youth one is on a silver plain, which grows more distant as one grows older.

3

Other familiar preoccupations of Rimbaud's emerge from the allegories, although these at first seem very different from the rest of the *Illuminations*. The key piece, "Conte," is a tale of frustration:

> Un Prince était vexé de ne s'être employé jamais qu'à la perfection des générosités vulgaires. Il prévoyait d'étonnantes révolutions de l'amour, et soupçonnait ses femmes de pouvoir mieux que cette complaisance agrémentée de ciel et de luxe. Il voulait voir la vérité, l'heure du désir et de la satisfaction essentiels. Que ce fût ou non une aberration de piété, il voulut. Il possédait au moins un assez large pouvoir humain.
>
> Toutes les femmes qui l'avaient connu furent assassinées. Quel saccage du jardin de la beauté! Sous le sabre, elles le bénirent. Il n'en commanda point de nouvelles. — Les femmes réapparurent.
>
> Il tua tous ceux qui le suivaient, après la chasse ou les libations. — Tous le suivaient.
>
> Il s'amusa à égorger les bêtes de luxe. Il fit flamber les palais. Il se ruait sur les gens et les taillait en pièces. — La foule, les toits d'or, les belles bêtes existaient encore.
>
> Peut-on s'extasier dans la destruction, se rajeunir par la cruauté! Le peuple ne murmura pas. Personne n'offrit le concours de ses vues.
>
> Un soir il galopait fièrement. Un Génie apparut, d'une beauté ineffable, inavouable même. De sa physionomie et de son maintien ressortait la promesse d'un amour multiple et complexe! d'un bonheur indicible, insupportable même! Le Prince et le Génie s'anéantirent probablement dans la santé essentielle. Comment n'auraient-ils pas pu en mourir? Ensemble donc ils moururent.
>
> Mais ce Prince décéda, dans son palais, à un âge ordinaire. Le Prince était le Génie. Le Génie était le Prince.

La musique savante manque à notre désir.

This "prince," who may seem to be in the grip of romantic boredom, is really in a predicament very similar to Rimbaud's own in his rejection of ordinary life and his dissatisfaction with any but the perfect love. In killing the women of his loves he is strongly reminiscent of the poet of "Mes petites amoureuses." In the slaughter of his followers and his blooded animals, and the burning of his buildings, he would seem to be the victim of one of those destructive rages which now and then are expressed through Rimbaud's images of violence. (We have just seen Rimbaud invoke a cataclysm to purify the world of "Après le déluge." In the verse poem which begins "Qu'est-ce pour nous, mon cœur"—published by Mouquet with the *Derniers vers* of 1872 although the date has been contested—he invokes a holocaust upon the entire world, and adds, after the dream of satisfied rage is finished: "J'y suis, j'y suis toujours"; his discovery that nothing has happened, leaving him exactly where he was before, even more closely parallels the condition of the "prince.") The failure of the women, followers, and animals to remain dead is a major frustration.

We may be sure, accordingly, that the "prince" is Rimbaud's allegory of himself. But who is the "genius"?

What the "genius" makes possible is plain from what we have discovered about Rimbaud's "new language." An "amour multiple et complexe" cannot differ importantly from the "new love" experienced in visions. And the linking of "bonheur" with the adjectives for ineffable and unbearable identifies this happiness with the felicity of the trance states. When together they sink into "la santé essentielle," one recalls that health is very nearly a synonym for energy, strength, and the other qualities which the "new language" associates with love.

Another text further identifies this "genius." "Génie" makes him personify all the qualities necessary for the euphoria of n a superlative degree: he is both affection and the and, being described as "mesure parfaite et réin- also music, strength, health, and delight, and, just ntly for our understanding, a liberation from every-thing unlovely in the old life: "ces superstitions, ces anciens corps, ces ménages et ces âges." These redemptions operate from the very fact of his being. Moreover, when the coherent discourse of the first part of this text breaks up in the series of ejaculations of the second part, the poem falls twice into language which has now become especially significant:

> Son jour! l'abolition de toutes souffrances sonores et mouvantes *dans la musique plus intense!*
>
> O monde! et *le chant clair* des malheurs nouveaux!
>
> (The italics are mine.)

But in the allegory, both "prince" and "genius" die of their ecstasy—except that, as it turns out, only the "genius" fails to survive and the "prince" ultimately dies like anyone else. For, ends the story, "prince" and "genius" were the same man.

The "prince" has already been identified with the poet. Consequently, the "genius" can be nothing other than that side of the poet's personality which makes the poetry of the "Lettre du voyant" possible. He is the ego who is somebody else, the "JE" who is "autre." When he dies the poet returns to his first condition—ordinary life.

This text is obviously a commentary on the idea of poetic voyancy and another premonition of the ultimate failure of Rimbaud's enterprise.

The other allegory, "Royauté," also treats the poet's central experience, and once more foretells defeat. The couple who, one morning, want the lady of the pair to be made queen, are again the two parts of the personality. Their "testing"—the preparation of the poet for his vision—has been accomplished.

They become "royal," but for one day, and here the vision breaks off. We may read this as meaning that momentarily the poet's soul (feminine, like the queen) reaches the state it wants, but that this triumph is temporary.

What the allegories say, in summary, is that Rimbaud's doubts still haunt him. The discovery that he has not done what he had hoped with poetry will not catch him by surprise.

That he is aware of the danger of having to return to the life of ordinary men, much as he hates it, is already evident in "Conte." In "Matinée d'ivresse," in which the fanfare of music accompanies his vision, he foresees that it will shortly give way to what he calls "l'ancienne inharmonie"; this has to be the opposite of the vision: ordinary, everyday existence. In the text called "Being beauteous" he dramatizes a struggle between two musics, one "sourde" and muted, the other "rauque" and harsh.

> Devant une neige un Être de Beauté de haute taille. Des sifflements de mort et des cercles de musique sourde font monter, s'élargir et trembler comme un spectre ce corps adoré; des blessures écarlates et noires éclatent dans les chairs superbes. Les couleurs propres de la vie se foncent, dansent, et se dégagent autour de la Vision, sur le chantier. Et les frissons s'élèvent et grondent, et la saveur forcenée de ces effets se chargeant avec les sifflements mortels et les rauques musiques que le monde, loin derrière nous, lance sur notre mère de beauté, — elle recule, elle se dresse. Oh! nos os sont revêtus d'un nouveau corps amoureux.
>
> * * *
>
> O la face cendrée, l'écusson de crin, les bras de cristal! Le canon sur lequel je dois m'abattre à travers la mêlée des arbres et de l'air léger!

Rimbaud's "Being of Beauty" may remind some readers of Baudelaire's "Beauté," but Baudelaire's is supernaturally calm and unaffected by human turbulence, whereas the figure in Rimbaud's text is agitated and moves constantly. Beyond this, and possibly because of this, the reader learns little about her. She is superbly fleshed; she is a "Vision"; and she is "our Mother of Beauty." But she is also in the process of some kind of transformation — or is appearing differently to the beholder from second to second: she rises, broadens, and trembles "like a specter." About her is a play of light, as the colors "which go with life itself" change against the white background.

The vision suffices to put the poet in an ecstasy. She is "this adored body" and his bones feel clothed in a "new, amorous body." We know this language: this new and loving body is near enough to the "new love" of which we have heard elsewhere for us to recognize his state of beatitude. But the state is extremely transitory. After the climactic declaration the text breaks.

Everything mixes in one tremendous whirl. There is the final glimpse of the face, the torso and the arms of the vision, then the tangle of the trees and the "light air" and the "cannon." Either the beholder has fallen from some height or collapsed with vertigo. The cannon, on which he will come down, has been taken by some readers to be a real piece of artillery, used by some hostile agency to inflict the "scarlet and black wounds." This reading seems to me farfetched; the beholder's response to the vision has been erotic, and the reference is probably to the physical manifestation of it. But it is no less true that struggle, and an assault, are elements of the vision.

It is perfectly clear in the text that the figure of Beauty is under attack from "the world far behind" the witness, and that "raucous music" is associated with the aggression. The reference to music earlier in the piece is harder to read. Like the other, it is accompanied by the hissing — or whistling — of death. But this earlier music is mute, spreading in visible circles like ripples on water — and causing the movement of the figure which has been noted. From what Rimbaud says about music and new harmony elsewhere I am inclined to assign the first music to his response to the vision, the second to whatever destroys it, that is, the world outside the experience of the *voyant.*

In any event, it is clear that the world of literal life has prevailed over the vision and dissipated it—and since this is the text, among all the *Illuminations,* in which he tries to state the content of what he has seen, the dissipation may be particularly significant. For what has happened here is what has happened over and over again in his poems; the image that embodies his delight and joy, the object of his ecstatic contemplation, has refused to stay and be contemplated.

It is not clear that this particular vision is recorded as a failure. But the fact of its sudden collapse is enough to keep us from assuming that it was a success.

4

That there are poems of sheer euphoria among the *Illuminations* is unquestionable. "Phrases," the text which at the end sees him turning toward the shadows beyond his bed and invoking the company of his "filles" and "reines," belongs to the category. The first of the eight separated paragraphs imagines the usual couple—"we, the two faithful children"—whom it would be easy to identify with the dual personality of the poet, except that at the end of the paragraph the "I" is promising enigmatically to kill the "you." They are in a world reduced to a beach, a black wood, and a house—which is a house of happiness, one gathers, since it is described as "musical." But possibly we should understand that these things have now only been imagined, since the statement is clear that the murder will ensue when they shall have come to be.

The second paragraph talks about being strong (with the force, energy, essential health, one feels in the euphorias?) and ends with the declaration that the speaker can never discard love. The third part reproaches the "you" of the couple, who is apparently a female—his soul, we remember, was a woman in

"Royauté"—for her indifference and begs for her company, which is the one comfort available in all this vile despair. And in the next part, without warning, we have moved into an interior scene where there is a smell of ashes in the air and of wood sweating in the fireplace, of wilted flowers carried home from walks, and of the mist of canals in open fields. One is at a loss to find the relationship of this to what has preceded; as a guess, the "you" has indeed saved him from despair.

For the next paragraph is a cry of sheer joy: "J'ai tendu des cordes de clocher à clocher; des guirlandes de fenêtre à fenêtre; des chaînes d'or d'étoile à étoile, et je danse." It would be hard to find in poetry a more complete expression of ecstatic excitement. And we know already how the poem ends.

One has no difficulty in classing this among the euphorias, and in the subcategory of the poems in which he is dealing with his emotion rather than with what causes it. But it must also be added that the poem is breathless and among the more incoherent pieces of a difficult collection. We know more from the fact that Rimbaud is drawing upon the words associated with euphoria in his "new language" than we do from any statement he makes with them.

The style of "Barbare" is somewhat less discontinuous:

Bien après les jours et les saisons, et les êtres et les pays,

Le pavillon en viande saignante sur la soie des mers et des fleurs arctiques; (elles n'existent pas.)

Remis des vieilles fanfares d'héroïsme—qui nous attaquent encore le cœur et la tête—loin des anciens assassins—

Oh! Le pavillon en viande saignante sur la soie des mers et des fleurs arctiques; (elles n'existent pas.)

Douceurs!

Les brasiers, pleuvant aux rafales de givre,—Douceurs!—les feux à la pluie du vent de diamants jetée par le cœur terrestre éternellement carbonisé pour nous.—O monde!—

(Loin des vieilles retraites et des vieilles flammes, qu'on entend, qu'on sent,)

Les brasiers et les écumes. La musique, virement des gouffres et choc des glaçons aux astres.

O Douceurs, ô monde, ô musique! Et là, les formes, les sueurs, les chevelures et les yeux, flottant. Et les larmes blanches, bouillantes, — ô douceurs! — et la voix féminine arrivée au fond des volcans et des grottes arctiques.

Le pavillon . . .

Numerous interpreters have felt that the opening line suggests an experience of the world more extensive than Rimbaud is credited with having at the time of composition, and it is tempting to assume that we have been wrong about the date when he wrote this text. Had he written this after *Une Saison en enfer,* nothing would hinder our assuming, further, that he had not finished it until after his trip to Java. He would have seen not only seasons and days, but volcanoes, much of the sea, and even the British jack (if this is what we are supposed to recognize in the bloody-meat red of the "pavillon"). But the assumption that the piece reflects personal experience is not indispensable and the temptation to make it should probably be resisted.

The sentences in question may simply mean that after much moving about in France and England, not necessarily in Java, one may still enjoy moments of perfect felicity, even though one is disappointed in hashish-taking as a means of seeing things, such as the arctic flowers, which do not exist. Whatever the scene of the vision, everything in it is pleasant — as the cry "Douceurs!" with which the poem is periodically interrupted, would tend to confirm. He could well be sitting by a brazier in some café, watching the dying ashes on the fire being lifted off by the cold draft. The sparks could look like a rain of diamonds, and the word "diamonds" has been used elsewhere

("Angoisse"), as has also the exclamation which accompanies it, "O monde" ("Génie"), in association with words we have identified as belonging to his special language. The parenthetical paragraph, with its remark about distance from the old "retreats," may refer to time past and ambitions renounced: in spite of the renunciation he still feels the old beatitude. The ashes are whirling off the fire like spray. He hears the music which we have come to expect him to hear in moments of ecstasy, and simultaneously sees—or, perhaps more accurately, feels—images which could have meaning only in the euphoric trance: "virement des gouffres et choc des glaçons aux astres." These turning "gulfs" are reminiscent of the vertigo we have suspected at the end of "Being beauteous," and the "shock" of icicle against star reminds us of the flames and ice which attend the supreme delight in "Matinée d'ivresse." And all this in turn is followed by a phrase which links the repeated exclamation, "Douceurs," with "monde" and "musique," preceding a final evocation of female figures and their attributes.

In other words, nothing in the poem except the hermetic reference to the volcanic fires in the heart of the earth requires more travel than, at most, a visit to England. Even the subterranean fires may refer only to the live coals deeper in the brazier, burning to keep "us" warm, and thus "carbonized for us." The interest of the piece lies less in geography than in the usefulness of knowing Rimbaud's private language.

This is, perhaps, the most relaxed and joyously visionary of all the *Illuminations*. It is, certainly, the only one which promises to continue; the phrase at the end picks up the beginning, as if in a round.

5

There are additional *Illuminations*, also, in which Rimbaud is again speaking of himself and his ambitions in poetry, and sounding as if in spite of his discouragement he has at least occasional, moderate hopes of success. "Jeunesse" refers to the "inevitable descent from heaven" and develops the theme of the great charm of childhood as compared with being adult; he feels that now he has aged until he is no more than "a dance and a voice"—and means that being only this is not being much. For the "instinctive voices" are exiled; "tunes and forms" are dead. But, despite this waning of powers, he does not feel—at least at the moment of writing this text—that his development is at a definitive end. "You are only at the point of the temptation of Anthony," he exclaims to himself.

Nothing important depends on whether or not at this point he had read Flaubert's book, or on his having seen or not seen the paintings of Breughel or Hieronymus Bosch. His remark is intelligible enough if we understand that, like the demons to the old monk, doubts and fears were coming to torture him, to make him give up the struggle toward what, for him, was the equivalent of salvation. In this there is no implication of his having given up. "You will get on with this work," he tells himself, and he speaks also of "all the possibilities of harmony and architecture."

But he is also capable of moods of deep depression.

Pieces like "Solde" sound as if he would be willing to abandon everything. "Guerre" is not far from being a statement of capitulation. Students who have not been convinced by Bouillane de Lacoste are skeptical of his views, fundamentally, because the tone of such texts coincides with the disappointment, and even black despair, which they find in *Une Saison en enfer*. In their view, *Une Saison en enfer* is not merely a comment on the *Illuminations* but also an attempt to say more fully, and perhaps more intensely, what the latter work seems, at moments only, to be saying.

Accepting their argument, however, would be as much an

act of faith as accepting that of Bouillane de Lacoste. Doubtless a neat and tidy mind, of the type of which the French say that he "takes care of his biography," would have proceeded in such a manner; but a disorganized one, deeply committed to the irrational, under heavy psychic pressures and perhaps sick, may easily be imagined to have every sort of difficulty in disposing of anything so important in one final gesture; individual experience may even prompt the reader to believe that the most effective way to assure that one's mind will be haunted by any such preoccupation is, precisely, to make such a conscious effort to dismiss it. Nothing guarantees that Rimbaud did not go on dwelling on his failure for some years after *Une Saison en enfer.*

Often his voice is clearer, his style more continuous, his statement more explicit, in the *Illuminations* inspired by depression than in his more manic ones. To a reader who has not renounced all his normal reading habits, this fact may be an additional incitement to insist upon the ultimate importance of such pieces. But we know from the poems of the winter of confinement in Charleville that when Rimbaud was frustrated and unhappy he was frequently capable of greater clarity and explicitness than in times when he was occupied by his variety of the beatific vision. What we find in the *Illuminations,* in this respect, is nothing new.

Such considerations, on the other hand, are not an authorization to overlook a text like "Solde":

> A vendre ce que les Juifs n'ont pas vendu, ce que noblesse ni crime n'ont goûté, ce qu'ignorent l'amour maudit et la probité infernale des masses; ce que le temps ni la science n'ont pas à reconnaître;
>
> Les Voix reconstituées; l'éveil fraternel de toutes les énergies chorales et orchestrales et leurs applications instantanées; l'occasion, unique, de dégager nos sens!

A vendre les Corps sans prix, hors de toute race, de tout monde, de tout sexe, de toute descendance! Les richesses jaillissant à chaque démarche! Solde de diamants sans contrôle!

A vendre l'anarchie pour les masses; la satisfaction irrépressible pour les amateurs supérieurs; la mort atroce pour les fidèles et les amants!

A vendre les habitations et les migrations, sports, féeries et comforts parfaits, et le bruit, le mouvement et l'avenir qu'ils font!

A vendre les applications de calcul et les sauts d'harmonie inouïs. Les trouvailles et les termes non soupçonnés, possession immédiate,

Elan insensé et infini aux splendeurs invisibles, aux délices insensibles, — et ses secrets affolants pour chaque vice — et sa gaîté effrayante pour la foule.

A vendre les Corps, les voix, l'immense opulence inquestionable, ce qu'on ne vendra jamais. Les vendeurs ne sont pas à bout de solde! Les voyageurs n'ont pas à rendre leur commission de si tôt!

It must be clear that what is up for sale, as the text puts it, is his poetic program. This will be a clearance of the furniture of the "Lettre du voyant" and the poetry he has written since. Everything he has wanted to see exist — the opportunity of escaping the world of the senses, the "priceless bodies," the "unaccountable wealth," "reconstituted voices," "the orchestral and choral energies." We have seen music, energy, and love associated too often, elsewhere in the *Illuminations,* not to recognize his vocabulary. His remark as to "les applications de calcul et les sauts d'harmonie inouïs" can only refer to the planned ("raisonné") derangement of the senses fundamental to his program and to the surging harmonies which were to have been his visions. Whether or not the last lines should be taken as a statement attempting to negate what has been said just above them, there is no denying what he has had in his mind. "Solde" is a poem about abdication.

But the *Illuminations* are far from being a book which has failure for its only, or even its principal, subject. Rimbaud remains here very much the poet he was in the earlier poems, hopeful of great success but apprehensive of great failure. If there is a difference between then and now, it lies in the greater frequency with which failure, whole or partial, is recorded.

Undoubtedly, the failures had more than this one cause. Just growing up, for example, to the point of realizing that any such vaulting ambition as his must involve a certain share of self-delusion — the cause so bitterly identified in *Une Saison en enfer* — could be another. But it seems hardly possible that he would have been so greatly disturbed if the visions themselves had been more consistently satisfactory and if they had not been so unutterably fragile.

We know how fragile they were. "Being beauteous" attributes the collapse to the victory of the everyday world over the world of the poet's imagining — and it may be argued that there are strong overtones of the standard Romantic burden of the world's hateful incomprehension of the poet — but the fact of the collapse remains unaltered. Something similar takes place in "Ornières," in which the circus which has occupied attention gives place to a funeral procession. "Aube" ends with the simple statement that the "child" awakes at noon, with the implication that he wakes alone, the Goddess having vanished. In "Nocturne vulgaire" a shift of the draft, and in "Les Ponts" a change in the light, suffice to dissolve the vision. In several of the *Illuminations* Rimbaud uses the word "comédie" for what he imagines, and, once more, the notion of a stage show emphasizes impermanence.

6

"Les Ponts" is representative of a number of *Illuminations* in which — as earlier in poems like "Michel et Christine" — Rimbaud's private emotions do not intrude. He seems, rather, to be playing a game of staring at a scene until its elements dissociate themselves from each other before his eye. (A reader interested in the mechanics of vision may try the experiment himself, or may remember what has happened to the wallpaper of his sickroom during bouts of fever.) Such scenes as those in "Les Ponts," the two *Illuminations* called "Villes" and the one called "Promontoire," may be objectively real. Much effort has gone into researches intended to discover whether he was not, at a given moment, looking at the temporary buildings of an exposition, or whether, at another, he did not actually visit Scarborough. Such questions have their own inherent interest, especially for future editors of Rimbaud's work, but do not bring much aid and comfort to the reader intent on obtaining what to him seems a plausible reading of such poems. For whether Rimbaud is looking at, or remembering, a real scene, or looking at, or remembering, a picture he has seen, we get from the text not what the object was but what he has made of it.

Thus, "Les Ponts":

> Des ciels gris de cristal. Un bizarre dessin de ponts, ceux-ci droits, ceux-là bombés, d'autres descendant ou obliquant en angles sur les premiers, et ces figures se renouvelant dans les autres circuits éclairés du canal, mais tous tellement longs et légers que les rives, chargées de dômes, s'abaissent et s'amoindrissent. Quelques-uns de ces ponts sont encore chargés de masures. D'autres soutiennent des mâts, des signaux, de frêles parapets. Des accords mineurs se croisent et filent, des cordes montent des berges. On distingue une veste rouge, peut-être d'autres costumes et des instruments de musique. Sont-ce des airs populaires, des bouts de concerts seigneuriaux, des restants d'hymnes publics? L'eau est grise et bleue, large comme un bras de mer. — Un rayon blanc, tombant du haut du ciel, anéantit cette comédie.

Whatever the source of the suggestion that has come to the poet's mind, this is clearly a pictorial distortion built by effects of light. The gray-crystal of the sky implies a special and unusual lighting. The "strange design" of the bridges across the canal—some with little houses on them—is the central element of a picture which has an unusually deep perspective. As a guess, the "minor chords" which are said to "pass each other" and go away, may be suggested by cables strung across the scene with objects hanging from them in such a way that, to the half-closed eye, they look like the lines of a staff with notes. Or possibly the music is heard rather than seen, and comes from the band instruments—the red coat and the instruments are not visible enough for one to be sure. Meanwhile, the water is gray and blue and broad like an arm of the sea, and in the general tone is a suggestion of pleasure.

But then the light changes and the "show" is gone. From the word "comédie" one concludes that the poet has been quite aware of what he has been doing. With the shift of light values the scene has reintegrated itself and resumed the physical organization it had before his eye performed the work of dissociation. The mention of music has not been enough to make us think that there has been an epiphany; there has been momentary hallucination accompanied by pleasure.

In certain other texts, like the first of the two called "Villes," the hallucination is so complete that one has no idea what picture, or what reality, may have stimulated it. The scene, whatever it is, has been taken completely apart and reassembled; the city is one seen only in dreams. From what is said about music in it we gather that the vision is essentially pleasant: belfries are singing "the ideas of peoples," and from castles built of bone comes "unknown music." And again, this vision and the accompanying felicity have been dissipated. At the end he is asking "what good arms, what beautiful hour" will bring them back.

Most of the same observations are applicable to the second

"Villes" with, in addition, a note that here once more the vision takes shape under the light of a gray and somewhat special sky. This text offers another case of taking the external world apart and putting it back together differently, according to the needs of his imagination. The process, of course, is one almost invariably necessary in painting, and, as has been frequently remarked, this fact may indeed be responsible for one's feeling that Rimbaud is actually looking at a painting as he writes. In this instance he actually cries out, "What a painting!" The words need mean no more than that he realizes the painterly quality of what is before his mind's eye.

The lighting of "Métropolitain" is almost like certain El Grecos. In the first paragraph, which may suggest the foremost plane in a painting, boulevards of pink and orange sand cross each other and are peopled by "young and poor" families buying fruit, the whole being bathed in a "winy" light. We move on, however, to a second plane where, under a very sombre and ominous lighting from the fog and smoke in a low sky, there is a confusion of helmets, wheels, boats, and rumps of—presumably—horses. On still a third plane is a phantasmagoric country side with an arched bridge, faces lit by lanterns, vegetable gardens, an undine by a river, and luminous skulls showing among rows of peas. At this point we have passed completely into an enumeration which makes no effort at organization in space. The vision ends by making no pictorial sense whatsoever; it has stopped without ever having been completed.

7

When an emotion does emerge from one of the texts dealing with urban scenes, it is most often one of dissatisfaction, discomfort, anxiety—in short, the opposite of felicity. The city is the opposite of nature. In "Métropolitain," the crowd surges over a "désert de bitume"—and this wilderness of asphalt has a blackness not unworthy of William Blake. At the end of "Enfance," the speaker, no longer a child, is buried in some sort of cellarage, lower even than the sewers, above which are the houses, gathering fogs, and red and black mud. "Ville," another urban piece, is the most completely dispirited of such texts — such as could have found a place in *Une Saison en enfer*:

Je suis un éphémère et point trop mécontent citoyen d'une métropole crue moderne parce que tout goût connu a été éludé dans les ameublements et l'extérieur des maisons aussi bien que dans le plan de la ville. Ici vous ne signaleriez les traces d'aucun monument de superstition. La morale et la langue sont réduites à leur plus simple expression, enfin! Ces millions de gens qui n'ont pas besoin de se connaître amènent si pareillement l'éducation, le métier et la vieillesse, que ce cours de vie doit être plusieurs fois moins long que ce qu'une statistique folle trouve pour les peuples du continent. Aussi comme, de ma fenêtre, je vois des spectres nouveaux roulant à travers l'épaisse et éternelle fumée de charbon, — notre ombre des bois, notre nuit d'été! — des Érinnyes nouvelles, devant mon cottage qui est ma patrie et tout mon cœur puisque tout ici ressemble à ceci, — la Mort sans pleurs, notre active fille et servante, un Amour désespéré, et un joli Crime piaulant dans la boue de la rue.

The man who could write this was surely ready to describe his season in hell. One comes ultimately to the conclusion about the *Illuminations* that though in some of them Rimbaud is a poet of complete bliss and beatitude, in others he shows himself to be capable of one of the world's most eloquent pronouncements in dispraise of life. Of the major elements from which *Une Saison en enfer* is built, only one is missing — the savage, almost hysterical, self-laceration which is their hallmark.

Chapter X — From the Far Side of Despair

NOTHING could be more natural than that our time should have made Rimbaud one of its special heroes. We have been aware of ourselves as living in — perhaps living through — an age of anxiety, and identified him as typically anxious. The heroes of our fiction have been alienated figures, and we know that Rimbaud's alienation was deep. We have honored, above all, those who have shown themselves capable of pronouncing a total refusal of the world in which we have no choice but to live, and written down Rimbaud as one of the most exemplary of such *révoltés*. Discussions of his work as a "poetry of revolt" have abounded, especially since the brave days of Existentialism and the publication by Albert Camus of *The Rebel,* and the importance of *Une Saison en enfer* has been emphasized, at times out of proportion.

Revolt, once defined by Camus as the utterance of a universal No—example: Ivan Karamazov's rejection of a world made good by one child's suffering—is distinguishable from mere rebellion by its absoluteness, philosophical seriousness, and cosmic scope. The most cogent metaphysical statement is perhaps contained in André Malraux's demonstration, in *The Voices of Silence,* that the function of art has always been to express man's refusal of "the human condition." How Rimbaud—especially the Rimbaud "with the wind in his heels" of the various biographies—could have come to be seen as the ancestor of all who held such views is easy to understand. Had he not written a book which was a complete rejection of the world as he had known it? And had he not, having written it, followed word with deed, simply walking out and slamming the door definitively behind him? If he had not actually expressed the theory of revolt, he had, according to this view, furnished a classic example of the practice.

It can at least be said in favor of such a notion that, even if closer inspection reveals that Rimbaud fell rather short of being the model he has been said to be, his example made it considerably easier for the latter-day stereotype of the *révolté* to come into existence. But before more than this can be granted, certain critical distinctions are in order: we are not free to forget, though some have managed to do so, that Rimbaud himself speaks, in *Une Saison en enfer,* of never having understood "la révolte." That he was violently repelled at times by the world around him no one who can read would conceivably deny. He has looked on life and not found it invariably good. With so many poets of his time, from Hugo to Tennyson, he can imagine a rationally organized political future in which ordinary human beings would be allowed to realize their innate potentialities and a society in which love would replace greed and cupidity. Of this what he sees about him falls heartbreakingly short — as it falls short also of the world of the innocent child, who now is doomed to be contaminated and degraded by the mere process of growing up. Anyone could imagine something better, such as his imaginary "Orient," exempt from the devastation of commerce, industry, colonialism, and what his time thinks of as science. The effort of creating a more habitable world would not be great, even if the difficulty had been increased by the consciousness of accumulated guilts which apparently strike him as the principal heritage of a Christian society.

But this is only one of the several "visages" of Rimbaud which appear in *Une Saison en enfer*. This is also the youth who is at the end of his liaison with Verlaine, who begins his account of his personal hell just before, and finishes it just after, the shooting in Brussels. In addition, this is the poet who has staked so much on poetry and fallen far short of the goal; the failure half-foreseen in the "Lettre du voyant" has become a part of the reality in which he must manage to live. He has, finally, had the experience of the brink of insanity, to which he has been led perilously close by the practice of his method. The mixed nature of his spiritual and physical predicament, with the disaffections which turn inward as well as outward, radically complicates the question of Rimbaud's revolt.

2

Human life, as Sartre's Oreste was not the first to observe, begins on the far side of despair. Rimbaud's account of his spiritual experience follows him not only down through the Slough of Despond but up again on the far side and onto the firm ground beyond. This "collection of a few pages from the notebook of the Damned" does reveal a progress, however incoherent and tortured the account may be: it takes its reader from the utter despair of the earlier sections through to a mood of acceptance (however unwilling) and of reconciliation (at least partial). The impression that Rimbaud's intention, together with his feelings, underwent some modification while his book was in the writing is, almost certainly, well grounded: there may well have been a moment, after his break with Verlaine, when he could see no exit from his predicament, and another, subsequent one when some hope was once again possible. We may not, after all, neglect that he finally called his book a *Season,* after toying with such titles as *Livre païen* and *Livre nègre*; the characteristic of seasons is that they have a beginning and an end.

It is incontestable that places in *Une Saison en enfer* are expressions of complete revolt. But a review of the entire book leaves the feeling that the mood of revolt is not everywhere present and that it does not prevail in the end.

A majority opinion among Rimbaud specialists holds that the opening section is an introduction written after the shooting scrape in Belgium, and contains a preliminary statement of the major themes. The time had been, the text says, when everything was good, when all hearts were open and every wine flowed free, a time of a fine party—"un festin"—when, in short, he had been happy. But subsequently he had lost the "key" to the "festin" and had, so to speak, shot his albatross, by taking Beauty upon his knees and insulting her. Now, having realized his mistake *in extremis*—on the point of "the last quack," a possible allusion to what might have happened if Verlaine had been a better hand with firearms—he would like to find the "key" again. The key is charity, he says. But thinking that he can recover it is a delusion; Satan is there to tell him that he must remain a "hyena" to the end. So at the end of the passage he offers Satan his notes on the experience.

It is just as likely that the second section, "Mauvais sang," was written before the final visit to Verlaine which culminated in the shooting, or at least that it was conceived if not actually written before these events, since it alone contains the material which would justify his having written a friend about the titles he later discarded. Here Rimbaud is attributing his faults to his belonging to an "inferior race"—seeing himself at first as a descendant of the old, conquered Gauls and subsequently as a Negro in some distant country about to be colonized by Europeans. In either of these avatars he belongs to those who do not choose Christianity but have it forced upon them and become its prisoners. Momentarily his imagination plays with the idea of being born a true and complete pagan, ignorant of and thus unplagued by the ideas of good and evil and the "torments of the soul which is almost dead to the Good." But this vision dissolves like the previous ones and the section ends with an image of himself marching like a soldier into combat.

"Nuit de l'Enfer" is devoted to the reality of the hell where he now finds himself. Directly now, not through metaphors, he describes his plight. He is indeed a victim of Christianity in that, without being able to divest himself of his sins, he is still aware of them as sins and as condemning him to eternal punishment. If he seems relatively untroubled by the loss of heaven he is remarkably conscious of the pains of hell. This section is more intelligible to those who accept the hypothesis that after Verlaine shot him, Rimbaud, under the shock of having come close to death and at the same time seeing all his projects collapse entirely, went through a religious crisis which very nearly resulted in a return to the Catholic practices of his childhood.

In the following section, "Délires," he turns violently to self-accusation. The first of its two subdivisions, the celebrated "Époux infernal," the account of his life with Verlaine, uses the noteworthy literary strategy of giving the point of view to the other member of the couple. Verlaine is characterized by his voice, which is full of self-pity, nagging, and female weakness. He comes off poorly, a pitiable if not despicable picture. The technique lets Rimbaud appear as he imagines he must have looked to Verlaine, extraordinarily cruel and revoltingly sadistic, as well as perversely vicious. Rimbaud's judgment of himself is no less severe for being indirect. And the second subsection, "L'Alchimie du verbe," goes on, with the poet speaking in his own person, to condemn him as thoroughly as poet as he has been condemned just before as moral individual. There is a fair possibility that the second subsection was written before the first and before the rupture with Verlaine; it seems hardly possible, on the other hand, that the first can have been written before the two poets separated for good and all. Thus, if this assumption is correct, Rimbaud would first have contemplated reasons for the unsatisfactoriness of his poetry, and then have looked for the reasons in his own moral inadequacy.

But the "Orient" section, which follows next, turns attention from the defective poet to the defective world, setting up a contrast between an "Orient" which he imagines and an "Occident" which is the world he lives in and tolerates so little. This section has given encouragement to exegetes who, like Rolland de Renéville, interpret Rimbaud's poetry as implying close familiarity with Eastern philosophy. But what Orient is Rimbaud talking about? The whole subject remains vague. Actually, in the full thematic development of the *Saison,* what is important is less an East that never was than a West which the poet knows well and detests thoroughly. The East has negative virtues only: the absence of the "false elect," of a bourgeois society, of a Christianity which is also bourgeois, of western commerce and industry, art, and philosophy. We have returned, in other words, to the theme first stated in "Mauvais sang," and to a material which permits us to talk about a revolt against life. But here again, self-accusation complicates the picture: if only, he says, he had had the eyes to see the truth of all this while there was still time. And once again, for all his savagery, there is audible the faintest note of self-pity.

The themes now having been stated, and developed as far as they will ever be, Rimbaud returns to the violent, almost frenetic tone of "Mauvais sang," and in "L'Eclair" protests against the empty notion of salvation through work. He can admit that all human effort may not be vanity, and he recalls his moments of socialist idealism when the dignity of labor appealed to him, but he rejects the possibility of redemption by such effort as too slow. He puts the thought away along with his attempts to attain the Unknown, and also dismisses the solution of religion as a hangover from childhood. He simply does not want to die; he wants to go on and live his "twenty years," meaning the two decades he allows himself as a future. And if eternity is thus lost—a sarcastic final exclamation—so much for that!

Thus he comes to the point, in "Matin," of measuring his final degradation. The promise of youth, by whatever crime or error of his, has not been kept. Let anyone who will tell the story; he has, himself, passed beyond the limit of communication. "I no longer know how to speak." And yet, he continues, the story of his suffering is now finished. He has been through the real hell, the one, he insists, of which the Son of Man burst the gates. There is open before him a kind of vision of Bethlehem, with the star always before his eyes and the Magi of heart, soul, and spirit, together with the promise of a "new work, new wisdom, the confusion of tyrants, and the end of superstition." The section ends by picking up the theme of the "pagan" and "Negro" sections: "Slaves, let us not curse life." The tone is quieter now than it has been previously, and he mentions his lassitude.

In the final section, "Adieu," it is "already autumn," but why, he asks, regret a waning earthly sun when one is in search of a divine light? Yet autumn calls up a picture of intense suffering, and distress, followed by the thought that if this is bad, comfort is hardly better. He passes into a tone of resignation, and the words he uses are famous. "J'ai créé toutes les fêtes, tous les triomphes, tous les drames: J'ai essayé d'inventer de nouvelles fleurs, de nouveaux astres, de nouvelles chairs, de nouvelles langues. J'ai cru acquérir des pouvoirs surnaturels. Eh bien! je dois enterrer mon imagination et mes souvenirs!" And on this note of acceptance of his lot, with all this implies in respect to the themes which run through his book, his season ends. He had thought himself seer or angel, and created his own feasts and triumphs and dramas, a new nature, a new heaven, new bodies, and new languages; he has returned to earth, to the new duty he must find, with a harsh reality to embrace.

3

In order to make sense of these texts in their totality, one must be alert to their falling at times into a dramatic form: it should be recognized that Rimbaud is speaking here in more than one voice. If what he says means anything at all, he has been on the threshold of madness. There can be very little doubt of what kind of insanity he had contemplated so closely. "L'Alchimie du verbe" makes it abundantly clear that his visionary experiments had not been far from breaking his contact with the world in which men live and to which their dreams ordinarily refer. There can come a moment when the subject merely turns his face to the wall, refuses to know people around him, becomes unable to take food and finally succumbs to inanition. How close to the edge the author of the *Illuminations* actually came, in that moment when he was "waiting to become a dangerous madman," nobody can say, but he leaves no doubt that it was close enough to give him a severe fright. Thus it is no surprise to detect at times in the *Saison en enfer* one voice which is savage, sarcastic, ironic, and occasionally brutal, which keeps speaking up in the name of harsh reality — the reality which must at all costs be embraced, and which replies to the other voice, that of the poet-*voyant*.

Critics who from the internal evidence of the *Illuminations* and *Une Saison en enfer* tend to the persuasion that it is possible to divide Rimbaud's life as poet into sharply defined periods, are also fond of the idea that he went through a moment of violent hallucination and delusion during the spring of 1872, at the moment of the last inchoate poems in verse. It is true that his illustrations of his "madness," which he quotes in "L'Alchimie du verbe," are from these writings, but nothing proves that the time of the writing was his only one of precarious mental balance. Isabelle Rimbaud may not be the most dependable of witnesses, the best interpreter of her brother's poems or the significance of various events in his life, but there is little reason to think that what she says of his behavior during the writing of these pages in the attic of the farmhouse at Roche — the shouts and groans from above stairs, the unpredictable conduct and erratic moods — is an invention. The story is true because she would have no object in telling a false one: the struggle to keep a grip on reality was grim. Her story is confirmed by the texts themselves — which Isabelle long failed to realize that the world would ever read.

An example can be the evocation of childhood in "Nuit de l'Enfer," where his imaginations of hell are particularly vivid. "La peau de ma tête se dessèche. Pitié! Seigneur, j'ai peur. J'ai soif, si soif. Ah! l'enfance, l'herbe, la pluie, le lac sur les pierres, *le clair de lune quand le clocher sonnait douze* . . . le diable est au clocher, à cette heure. Marie! Sainte-Vierge!" (The italics are in the text.) This voice belongs to the hallucinated poet. To it the voice of the man in contact with reality answers abruptly and with impatience: "Horreur de ma bêtise."

One could be tempted to identify the two voices with the two parts of the divided personality of the "Lettre du voyant" — the "JE" who is "autre" and the "je" who is not. The first of the two speeches follows the then-and-now pattern familiar from some of the *Illuminations*: opposed to the frightening dryness of the infernal present are childhood and the sweetness of nature, and the moonlit sounds of the midnight belfry which have now been replaced by Satan. Thus, the second voice can be read as rejecting the "stupidity" of the poems — as well as that of the poet.

Another example occurs in the introductory passage. The poet has explained how he has lost the key to the great feast and sunk into various sorts of depravity; now, at the point of death, he would like to recover the key which is Charity.

> Or, tout dernièrement m'étant trouvé sur le point de faire le dernier *couac*! j'ai songé à rechercher la clef de l'ancien festin, où je reprendrais peut-être appétit.
>
> La Charité est cette clef.

So far, this is the voice of the *voyant,* desperately seeking salvation. But now the other voice interrupts: "Cette inspiration prouve que j'ai rêvé." Here again, and as always, the second voice is the voice of reality and sanity.

This technique is standard with Romantic ironists from Stendhal to Henri de Montherlant. "Aedificabo et destruam," writes Montherlant, "I shall construct, but to destroy." The procedure has nothing new for confirmed readers of Rimbaud. "And what about my job?" asks the voice of Nina at the end of "Les Réparties," and the down-to-earth question brings to an abrupt close that most detailed phantasy about love in a benevolent nature. At the end of "Roman," it will be remembered, the poet returns from flights of erotic reverie to the realization that he must look like something of a puppy. And though the words of "Le Cœur supplicié" speak of complete disgust with life, the lilting rhythm reminds us that the poet is conscious of being a bit too intensely eloquent for his years and stature. The same effect is produced in the poem that begins, "Qu'est-ce pour nous, mon cœur," when the poet emerges from a dream of global holocaust into an awareness that after all nothing has happened.

In *Une Saison en enfer,* each of the persistent themes—Christian religion, childhood, hostile external world, romantic travel, and so forth—occasions a renewal of the same treatment.

4

The religious crisis Rimbaud is supposed to have passed through in the hospital in Brussels is psychologically possible. Although his wound itself was minor, the experience of being shot was not. Rimbaud could have died without opportunity to confess his sins, do penance, and amend his life. To one brought up a Catholic, the thought is sobering. But the experience can only have sent him more precipitately along a way already chosen: he had begun *Une Saison* before this episode and is in a mood to examine his conscience.

Once he had committed himself to the ancient metaphor which equates suffering with the Nether Pit, he had almost no choice but to continue in the language of the Judaeo-Christian tradition. Suffering being hell, and hell being in turn punishment, the question, old as Job, arises inevitably: What have I done to merit this? The tone necessarily becomes one of self-recrimination and confession. Nothing could be less surprising than that readers like Claudel, Daniel-Rops, and Jacques Rivière, already predisposed to see every conflict stated in Christian terms, should have discovered in Rimbaud a kind of crypto-Catholic. To agree with them, however, requires resolute inattention to the contexts of the passages that they cite most often in defense of their view.

If there is any validity to the claim, put forth above, that the *Saison* frequently falls into the form of a dialogue between two voices which are both the poet's, then it must be significant that the voice that is aware of the claims of reality intervenes most often when the other voice has embarked on the subject of salvation through religion. In the introduction, Charity appears to be represented as the key to the lost "feast," but it is not entirely true that at that point the poet represents himself as having lost two of the three theological virtues: while he has been through a period of despair, *part* of him lives in hope of finding his key again; and it is now that the other voice denies the hope, telling him that he will always remain the "hyena." We may conclude from this that the religious urge is only one velleity among others. And each time the Christian solution is mentioned in the pages that follow, this conclusion is reconfirmed; the voice of reason and reality reminds him that he is losing the indispensable contact.

Throughout Rimbaud's confession such phrases occur as the famous: "I await God with *gourmandise*," an expression more easily understood by those familiar with the language of Catholic mysticism and the doctrine of transubstantiation. (Saint Teresa of Avila is known to have preferred the largest possible hosts at communion.) "God is my strength," he declares in another place, "And I praise God." No more is required to send those who are predisposed to do so off on an orgy of rereading the *Illuminations*, to make such discoveries as that the "Génie," otherwise identifiable with the *voyant* side of the poet's personality, is really Jesus Christ. But even those of such readers who are willing to admit that Rimbaud reveals himself to them as a Christian only upon fleeting occasion are bound to encounter very serious obstacles.

Rimbaud's cry about waiting for God with *gourmandise* is followed in the next sentence by the statement that he belongs "to an inferior race throughout eternity," and the ellipsis between the two declarations can hardly be filled by anything but a statement of causal relationship, either "because" or "consequently." The often quoted: "De profundis, domine," in "Mauvais sang," is followed immediately by words less often cited: "Am I stupid!" The words following his remark in "L'Eclair" about the odor of incense coming so strong to his bed in the hospital are to the effect that he recognizes "in this the filthy education of my childhood."

In texts written, most likely, both before and after the shooting, he associates Christianity with the idea of an inferior race. His feeling that he descends directly from the old Gauls, with all their bad habits and their vices, including laziness, seems less incongruous when one remembers that he was a contemporary of determinists like Taine. As one of the conquered people, he sees himself in a series of atavistic incarnations: pilgrim, leprous beggar, foot soldier, all playing subordinate roles, never members of the "councils." And historically, he reminds himself, the Gauls did not exactly seek Christianity, but had it forced upon them by their conquerors. At the same time, God is the refuge of the inferior.

When he sees himself not as a son of old Gaul but as a Negro in a country about to be invaded by Europeans, the connecting theme is inferiority. The whites come ashore, the cannon fire: one must submit, dress oneself in clothes, go to work. Not even those most persuaded of Rimbaud's Catholicism will argue that such a page constitutes a cry of Christian triumph. To accept Christianity, in this purview, implies an irrevocable admission not only of defeat but of one's having been defeated from the start. His playing with the idea that if one is genuinely exempt from all the inhibitions of a Christian civilization one is better off constitutes another flight from reality. The reader who submits scrupulously to the meaning of the total work recognizes that occasional velleities of submission and acceptance are counterbalanced by velleities of rejection.

The general theme persists in "Nuit de l'enfer," and in an even more desperate tone. He is trapped in his Christian tradition, the "slave of his baptism." He has had the vision of peace and bliss which would go with reconciliation to his faith: "Millions of charming creatures, a suave spiritual concert, strength and peace, noble ambitions, and so forth." But here the paragraph ends. The new one, which consists only of a repetition of "noble ambitions," but this time written with an exclamation point, can only be read as ironical: the voice of sanity has intervened again to collapse the vision; one who has been trained a Christian must live with what he has learned in his catechism; only the true, born pagan is safe from hell; the poet's parents have wrought his misfortune as well as their own.

And at the end of the book, in "Matin," in spite of the references to the star, the desert, and the Magi, the "Noël on earth" he speaks of is surely not the Christian one. New work and new wisdom, flight of tyrants and demons, and an end to superstition, go well of course with the idea of peace to men of good will — but these are men whose ideal of good will is, most likely, the far off, divine event of nineteenth-century idealistic socialism. The acceptance which the last pages of Rimbaud's book may be said to breathe is not an acceptance of Christianity. He is talking, rather, about a world which would be of a quality such that he would not feel himself preternaturally alienated from it.

What makes Rimbaud seem, at moments, so close to Christianity is, more than anything, his capacity for self-accusation. But in the last accounting, even this leaves one a bit suspicious. The very violence of the language he uses to call himself a fool, a knave, and a scoundrel has a touch of masochism about it. There is too good a chance that this self-laceration brings satisfactions and reliefs of its own. To be a fool and a failure is not, of itself, a sin. The frustration which comes from knowing that one has failed and been foolish can be as real as any other. Rimbaud, as we know, had the habit of lashing out when he was frustrated and does so now, when the source of the trouble is inside himself. Religion need not enter the discussion at this point. He may still be, quite simply, the young poet who tolerated nothing that came between him and felicity.

5

The world Rimbaud seems to have wanted would have had to be entirely different from the one he was in. He knows that in this present one the inferior race has inherited the earth. The last century has seen, he says, the victory of the People, of reason, of the nation, of knowledge. But knowledge — science to his contemporaries — seems to be nothing more than medicine, which is the codifying of old wives' remedies, and philosophy, which is the rearrangement of the sentiments of popular songs. For progress he has only scorn. "We are headed for the conquest of matter by mind," he declares, and the irony emerges as it develops that in his visions the priests and professors are always opposed to him. The leaders of the modern world — merchants, magistrates, generals, and emperors — are "faux nègres," he says, inspired by fever and cancer. It would be best to quit this continent and go off to "the true kingdom of the children of Cham" and, like them, be a cannibal. He gives to the devil the martyrs, the art, the inventions, and the ardor of those he calls the "pillagers" — his fellow Europeans. These aggressively commercial proprietors own everything, including Christianity.

To the characteristic delusions of the West, that nothing is vain, that knowledge is progress, and that work is good, he remains closed: no subterfuge can hide the fact that the trouble with the workaday world is work, the progress of the snail toward something which will never take place. The glimpses of the great modern city, probably London, are again — as in the *Illuminations* — reminiscent of Blake.

Rimbaud is no more specific on the world he detests than on any other of the half-dozen subjects which preoccupy him in *Une Saison*. Whether or not it is true that he now has no gift for description, as he says on the opening page, he clearly has no desire to describe. As always, his focus is not on objects but on his feeling about them. He wants no part of this world he finds about him; it makes him ill and all his instinct is to reject it. Yet he also has to face his situation: this world is a part of the reality which he must bring himself, at the end, to embrace. For the sake of his sanity and perhaps of his life he must accept it, though we may remember that to embrace is not always, and necessarily, a sign of love.

The opening pages of this book, plus the happy tone of some of the *Illuminations* in which the visions are reminiscences of childhood, has led some readers to believe that the *Saison* should be read as a rejection of the *adult* world and an expression of the wish to return, or regress, to childhood. In favor of this view, there is ample evidence in the *Illuminations* that as Rimbaud got older some early moment in life looked increasingly attractive to him. But on the other hand, the more one examines his biography, the harder it is to find any moment in his own life which would fit the description.

The children in his poems are not particularly happy either. Those in "Les Etrennes des orphelins" are in a pitiable plight; the group in "Les Effarés" are poor and cold. Those in the more autobiographical poems, "Les Poètes de sept ans," and "Les Premières Communions," are abjectly wretched. The only happy figure in Rimbaud's poems, actually, is the young poet who has momentarily contrived an evasion either through a real life fugue or through one of the imagination. And the author of *Une Saison en enfer* is by no means persuaded that the author of "Ma bohème" was on the road to happiness. "Ah, the life of my childhood, the open road in every weather, naturally sober, caring less than the best of beggars, proud of having neither country or friends, what stupidity it was!"

On the whole, it seems more likely that childhood appeared to him less as a specific refuge than as a time when, innocence and purity not having been contaminated by a specific vice, he had not departed on a course of scattering his talent to the winds. In a sense, *Une Saison en enfer* repeats the burden of the "Chanson de la plus haute tour":

Oisive jeunesse
A tout asservie,
Par délicatesse
J'ai perdu ma vie.

Rimbaud seems considerably more willing than some of his admirers have been since to face the fact of his vice. In the fugitive piece called "Les Déserts de l'amour," he is entirely explicit: "Not having loved women — though full of blood — his soul and heart, his strength, were brought up in strange errors." The author of the "Délires" chapter and of the *Illumination* called "Vagabonds," hard as he may be on poor Verlaine, does not spare himself.

But his vice is not his only reason for looking on his own character with disgust. He speaks of others: his proneness for anger and his delight in immorally soft living, his laziness and his lying. Here, as usual, he veils his terms and it is hard to know what he means in every case. It is not surprising if his experiments in voyancy put his nerves in a state such that he was subject to flare-ups of very bad temper; on the other hand, he and Verlaine were always so short of money that it is hard to imagine what experience he had of sybaritic living. Lying, since the French "mensonge" includes the lie which is lived as well as the lie which is told, may refer to the whole quality of his life during these years.

We do know what he meant by laziness. Rimbaud had never had any patience with work. Back in 1871 his mother had left him both frightened and indignant with her threats to make him get a job. He was always instinctively orthodox on this point: work was the primeval curse laid upon the race. His momentary exaltation over human labor was probably an expression of his sympathy for the laboring class during the months when he was intent on joining the Commune, rather than a personal commitment to toil. He says that he has all the laziness of the old Gauls, and part of his horror at discovering himself to be a member of the inferior race he connects with the state of being a slave: slaves are condemned to work.

We may wonder whether, in addition, he meant that he had not done faithfully the work of the poet. It is true that, unless there is poetry written in the interval of which we know nothing, he had done relatively little since mid-1872. As compared with Verlaine, at least, he had not much to show. But the conclusion is ours alone, and one which he does not endorse, that the practice of voyancy gradually incapacitated him for poetry.

In any case, along with all the other reasons for his self-revulsion there is the paramount one that, from his angle, the great experiment of voyancy had not succeeded. No document connected with modern French poetry is more often cited than "L'Alchimie du verbe." It has been taken as a faithful report of what he had been trying to do ever since the letter to Demeny. This is reasonable so long as the report is recognized as retrospective, and as an explanation of what he had meant in the letter itself. He is certainly saying that, looking back upon it, his enterprise was a great mistake. The attempt to induce hallucinations resulted in nothing more than induced hallucinations. The "sacred disorder of his mind" had given the world nothing that was not paltry. The project of tapping the irrational sources of poetry turned out to have been an immense, nearly fatal, self-deception.

But he exaggerates, somewhat, the case against his own work. Looking back over the poems in verse of 1872, one simply does not find the trace of all the trivialities which he says fascinated him during his period of disorder. Nor does one find them in the prose *Illuminations,* whenever it may be that these were written. Where, for example, is the evidence of his pleasure in church Latin, except possibly in the *Saison* itself? There is disagreement as to how much of his poetry he includes in his condemnation. The traditional view, that he had in mind everything he had ever written, has given way to one which has at least the merit of not going miles beyond what "L'Alchimie du verbe" actually says: it holds that he was saying farewell only to the *kind* of poetry which was to have been the glory of the "voyant." But this opens new questions.

Either we have to believe that this impulsive young man, having had his great inspiration no later than May 15, 1871, waited almost a year to explore the possibilities of hallucination, or else that he condemned virtually all his poetry written before the *Saison.* A year in the accelerated life of Rimbaud is the equivalent of a cycle in that of almost any other poet. Moreover, the *Saison* itself confirms what one gathers elsewhere about his impatience when moved by an impulse. And we have seen that some of the poems written within short months after the "Lettre du voyant" are more easily interpreted if one presupposes the practice of the program it sets forth. Moreover, we know that by June 10, 1871, he was urging Demeny to burn all the early poems which subsequently went not into the fire but into the "Collection Demeny." The request suggests strongly that the poet was persuaded of the superior value of poems of a new sort; and poems like "Le Cœur supplicié" and "Voyelles," whatever the present estimate of their value, already reveal an irrationality which has yet to be proved *not* to be the result of applying the famous method. The thesis advanced in an earlier chapter, that the "Bateau ivre" is a report on systematically contrived hallucinations, is not widely supported by respected experts in the subject, but the evidence stands by itself. No one contests that in Roche, in 1872, Rimbaud brought on himself a crisis which frightened him considerably—even though the evidence is nothing more than a line left in one of his drafts—but this makes it no easier to concede that his renunciation in "L'Alchimie du verbe" applies only to a very small part of his total output.

The poems which he sprinkles through this chapter are, obviously, the work of 1872, and mostly of the first half of that year. But he also condemns "Voyelles" as a characteristic product of his enterprise, and this poem is surely earlier. That he now scorns the poems of 1872 is very likely, since either he does not go to the bother of copying them into his new work in correct form or else quotes them defectively on purpose. But this does not have to mean that only these poems were included in his condemnation.

It should be remembered that Rimbaud was in the habit of abandoning his poetry. The injunction to Demeny was a formal act, covering the poems up to that time. The sudden cessation, about a year later, of the flow of poems in syntactically solid verse would seem to be a second, this time informal, renunciation. *Une Saison en enfer* now appears as the third in a series, almost indicative of a habit. The fact that he does not specifically include in his renunciation the prose *Illuminations* may be taken to confirm Bouillane de Lacoste's view that these last had not been written, or may, on the other hand, simply show that in 1873 Rimbaud did not recognize that the texts formed a unified collection. Everything testifies that Rimbaud had no objections to publishing his work; it seems likely that in 1875, when he wanted to recover the manuscripts from Verlaine, his intention of sending them to be printed was very real. The possibility that Rimbaud did not repudiate the prose *Illuminations* simply because he was not aware that there was anything there to repudiate is not entirely to be dismissed.

Everything considered, however, we may as well assume that Rimbaud's declaration regards only the poetry he has written up to 1873—whatever may be included in this list. It does not constitute a promise never to write poetry again, and cannot be considered a general farewell to the activity of writing. Rimbaud is simply giving up writing a kind of poetry which he has now outgrown, just as he had done once before in his life and quite possibly twice. Few poets have not had moments of discouragement when they felt that their work to date amounted to less than nothing, and yet not hoped, perhaps without daring to say so, that in future they might yet realize their promise.

The scandal of *Une Saison,* if scandal there is, lies in Rimbaud's having been so willing to abandon poems which must be counted, by any standard, among the finest in French poetry. Here at last the Romantic has been divorced from the oratorical and the grand manner (which had hampered Baudelaire and sometimes Gérard de Nerval) and is not inferior to the best English and German Romanticism. It is a pity that Rimbaud did not know it.

But he is now very completely trapped in a machine of his own making. Poetry—at least his poetry—now takes its place as a means of eluding "harsh reality." Among other ways of doing so are those pictured in the visions of the *Saison,* in which he sees himself hardened by travel and adventure. These are often brought forward by interpreters who neglect to add, because they do not notice, that these things are introduced into the book only so that Rimbaud can reject them.

One of these is the celebrated "prophecy" of his own future: "I have put in my time. I am leaving Europe. The sea air will burn my lungs; far climates will bronze me . . . I shall return with iron muscles, skin darkened, fury in my eye: by my features people will take me for one of the strong race. I shall have gold, and be lazy and brutal. Women care for these strange invalids who are back from the hot countries. I shall have a hand in politics. Saved!" Biographers like Berrichon and Madame Maléra have been tremendously impressed by this passage and, by such devices as harmlessly increasing the total of Rimbaud's savings in Abyssinia, have made it sound like an uncanny prevision of what actually happened to him. But it is the voice of the *voyant* which has taken over the dialogue here. There is a break in the text in a moment, and then the voice speaks which values reality: "One does not leave." This vision is herewith rejected just as he had rejected Christianity, and just as he had rejected the method when it did not lead to happiness. There is no escape.

The more one ponders this enigmatic text, the more one has trouble believing that escapes were what Rimbaud felt he needed, and the harder it becomes, accordingly, to read *Une Saison en enfer* as the preface to a departure for Abyssinia. So far as the testimony of the book goes, he has come to see that he is engaged, as he had thought long ago he might be, in an unsuccessful enterprise. Now he admits the truth and, at the end of the book, is ready to go on living.

This does not sound like the work of a poet in revolt so much as it sounds, as does everything else he wrote, like the work of a very great poet.

Chapter XI — The Poem as Secret

NOT ALL of Rimbaud's poems have been discussed here, because a number do not appear to be relevant to the discussion. Some find no place because they merely corroborate the statement that though the poet's own felicity—or the absence of it—was his major preoccupation it was by no means his only one. I have no wish at all to deny the interest of pieces like "Fêtes de la faim," the phantasy on hunger which he apparently wrote in London when he and Verlaine were not eating regularly, but I would argue, vehemently, that this poem is calculated to fascinate the psychoanalyst more than anyone else and that it does not involve considerations important to the present context. I should also put in the same category, though for somewhat different reasons, the poems of the "Stupra," including the notorious "Sonnet du trou du cul";

they seem to me principally to be indications of how far Rimbaud would go, at the moment of writing, to attract attention to himself.

A number have been omitted because they only bear out what has already been made evident by other poems. Once it has been established, for example, that one of the sources of Rimbaud's frustration was the political aftermath of 1870, there would seem relatively little point in analyzing "Orgie parisienne, ou Paris se repeuple." In it Rimbaud opens the vials of his wrath upon the population of the city which, when danger has passed, returns to take up its sordid, everyday concerns; he does so with superior eloquence; but we have had ample experience, elsewhere, of his lashing out at what makes him unhappy.

For the same reasons I have also passed over the various prose pieces which have been discovered from time to time and hailed with unvarying excitement. From "Un Cœur sous une soutane" through the so-called "Proses évangéliques" these seem to teach us little about Rimbaud's habitual behavior. They have their special interest, because they are Rimbaud's, but if his name were not attached to them it is doubtful that they would attract even passing notice.

Finally, a small handful have been omitted from consideration because of my own hesitations as to how to treat them. For example, "Entends comme brame":

Entends comme brame
près des acacias
en avril la rame
viride du pois!

Dans sa vapeur nette,
vers Phœbé! tu vois
s'agiter la tête
de saints d'autrefois . . .

Loin des claires meules
des caps, des beaux toits,
ces chers Anciens veulent
ce philtre sournois . . .

Or ni fériale
ni astrale! n'est
la brume qu'exhale
ce nocturne effet.

Néanmoins ils restent,
— Sicile, Allemagne,
dans ce brouillard triste
et blêmi, justement!

The wisest word yet said about this piece comes from one of Rimbaud's editors, who wonders whether any sense whatsoever is to be made of it. The "rame" in question is the stick used to support growing peavines. "Bramer" means to bellow like certain animals. The effect is, to say the least, Daliesque. And one searches in vain for any way of making "nette," which applies only to something clean-cut and sharp of outline, modify vapor! It is, of course, possible that beneath the surface of the poem is a feeling of ineffable delight and happiness. If so, the word "ineffable" is to be emphasized. It is equally possible that the piece was written while Rimbaud was drunk. In any case, this nocturne can hardly be used as a clear example of anything whatsoever except one of the sources of an interpreter's bafflement.

2

Despite such exceptions, the remaining evidence seems ample. It shows us a very young poet who begins his career with repeated bids for attention, making the gestures toward a public, however small, which assume implicitly that a poem is a social act, performed for an audience. We have watched him, as time goes on, become increasingly difficult for any public to grasp, and at the end of his career—and here neither exact dates nor the relative order of publication of the *Illuminations* and *Une Saison en enfer* make a perceptible difference—his achievement is an utterance so private that the attentive reader feels almost indiscreet, as if he were guilty of prying into what is not properly his concern.

From the study of his creative habits we know how this came about. We have seen that the landscape of the poems of 1872, of which the poet speaks repeatedly without ever describing, is not before the eyes of the reader: Rimbaud refers to it, but does not describe. He assumes, so to speak, an audience with which he has lost direct contact. He cares more about his own feelings than of our knowing their sources. It is possible, however, to reconstruct something of this landscape because of the poet's recurrent mentions of the same features. But the prose *Illuminations* are so various and different from each other that such a reconstruction is not possible, and in *Une Saison en enfer,* though his referential procedure is familiar, his material is essentially psychological and moral, and we lack the reference points which would correspond to the châteaux and briars of his landscapes. We become eavesdroppers, very largely, on what is in essence a secret monologue.

We have also seen the development of his incoherence. There is almost universal agreement that it began with some decisive event in his life which took place during the spring of 1871, more or less at the time of the "Lettre du voyant," and the belief is widespread that the event was a homosexual encounter which shocked him deeply. Why this second conviction should be so general is not quite clear; nothing of the kind is needed to explain the subsequent development of his poetry. His discovery that the images of the visions which he conjured up according to the procedures mentioned in the letter tended to dissolve so rapidly could have been a fully sufficient cause of the increasing discontinuity of his language. Corresponding to the mobility and evanescence of the vision is the incoherent, exclamatory cry.

Doubtless it was to be expected that in such a situation the *Illuminations* should command so large a share of the attention of recent critics. They would probably have done so even without the added incentive provided by the recent discussion of the dates, which had the omnipresent implication that perhaps we would understand the texts better now that we were freed from certain possible presuppositions. "I alone hold the key to this savage parade," Rimbaud had written at the end of "Parades," and this declaration alone would suffice to keep criticism active.

This interest in the *Illuminations,* at the expense of the other poems, seems to me disproportionate. The verse poems of 1872 would appear as worthy of interest, and as great a challenge to the interpreter, and the nature of the critical activity would be the same. For, with both prose and verse, we come more and more to be occupied not with the allegedly total poem but with the fragmentary, lyric exclamation.

For example, our attention rivets upon the parenthesis which forms the second paragraph of the *Illumination* called "Angoisse": "(O palmes! diamant! – Amour, force! – plus haut que toutes joies et gloires! – de toutes façons, partout, – démon, dieu, – Jeunesse de cet être-ci: moi!)."

From what we know of the habitual language of the *Illuminations,* this is clearly a shout of ecstasy; everything is reasonably intelligible down to the exclamation "démon, dieu." From the context these words describe Rimbaud, but should we take him to mean them literally? Does he truly declare that he is superhuman? Or are they metaphor? And do "demon" and "god" mean the same thing to him, or does he mean that he is the two distinct personalities simultaneously? And does all this refer to his being, as he said he wished to make Verlaine also, a "son of the sun"? The questions multiply endlessly, and remain unanswered—and preoccupy us almost totally without reference to the reading of this text as an aesthetic whole.

The transcendent qualities which make Rimbaud the poet he is are present in the fragment. Almost every word in the passage is, to borrow the terms of the grammarians, "expressive"; "tool words," those which say little in themselves but define and control the meanings of the others, are largely absent; instead of syntax we have juxtaposition. Hence Rimbaud's concentration, and hence, also, since so few words perform discursive and thus prosaic functions, his poetic purity. The exclamatory nature of his expression, its nominal quality, the absence of verbs, the violence of the antithesis, and the elimination of every unnecessary syllable generate his intensity.

Such fragments are not exclusively characteristic of the prose *Illuminations*. From the winter of 1870–1871, they turn up everywhere in Rimbaud's work, flashes which blind the reader, almost, to the surrounding text:

> Et l'Aube exaltée ainsi qu'un peuple de colombes . . .
> Que pouvais-je boire dans cette jeune Oise,
> Ormeaux sans voix, gazon sans fleurs, ciel couvert . . .
> Voilà la cité sainte, assise à l'occident . . .

Or the superbly beautiful:

> L'Etoile a pleuré rose au cœur de tes oreilles,
> L'infini roulé blanc de ta nuque à tes reins;
> La mer a perlé rousse à tes mammes vermeilles,
> Et l'Homme saigné noir à ton flanc souverain.

To quote examples in this way is of course to insert a personal note in the discussion. But the reader who has followed it this far will not have done so without having personal, private responses to Rimbaud of his own which he may, if he wishes, profitably substitute for mine. These particular examples, however, are quoted because they come from the poems Rimbaud wrote even before he broke finally with everything in Charleville.

It proves nothing but the poverty of critical language that these may be referred to as fragments. Each, taken by itself, is as independent as a *haiku,* and as completely a whole. By their nature they are obscure as, we now incline to believe, all great poetry is obscure—beneath what superficial clarity it may happen to have. Thus, finally, Rimbaud breaks the long French tradition of a poetry which is marked, principally, by controlled, supervised, lucidly mellifluous, elegant eloquence.

In the ninety years since he fell silent we have become used to writers, in prose as well as verse, who have sought intensity and impact at the expense of clarity. Most recently, Albert Camus, in *The Stranger,* has been a master of parataxis: "Every sentence," says Sartre of this prose, "is an island." Gide, in *The Counterfeiters,* was determined that no chapter should profit from the momentum of the preceding one, and his declared object was a kind of purity which envisages a genre which is novel and nothing else in the sense that Rimbaud's work makes us conceive of a poetry which is nothing else. In Céline's *Journey to the End of the Night* the blurted narrative of his little hero, Bardamu, is intended, by its discontinuity, to be itself a protest against a world which does not make sense—and in its sequel, *Death on the Installment Plan,* normal punctuation at the ends of sentences is replaced by three-dot ellipses, to emphasize the absence of any connection between one sentence and the next. Ezra Pound, in his *Cantos,* obtains the ironic contrasts, by which his poem proceeds, through mere juxtaposition.

What may, in Rimbaud, have been largely involuntary thus

becomes one of several planned, self-conscious literary strategies. The difference between voluntary and involuntary is probably less important to us than the fact of our having come to accept such techniques of discontinuity—especially in writers whom we consider his successors in a "literature of revolt."

Our willingness to accept them may also prove to be a measure of the immense change which has taken place in our taste in poetry over the last century. We no longer require a poem to be, externally, an æsthetic unit, with the effect of its parts subordinated to the effect of the whole; we prefer flashes of insight to continuous expression, and we look for such flashes, especially, in poets whom we do not expect fully to understand. We want a poem capable of keeping from us at least a part of its secret.

Are we so disposed because of Rimbaud's influence, because of his having lived and written? Surely his work, more than that of Baudelaire and Gérard de Nerval, and indubitably more than Mallarmé's—whose discontinuities so often turn out to be disguised continuities—is oriented in the direction we have taken. Or is it, rather, that tastes which he had but a small part in forming now make him loom large in a very special perspective? Either is possible, but such questions are ultimately vain. The effort of asking them may be better spent in study which, though we know it will not dispel all the mysteries enshrouding it, may bit by bit increase Rimbaud's accessibility to us.

APPENDIX

BIBLIOGRAPHICAL NOTE

INDEX

Appendix — La Lettre du Voyant

I've decided to give you an hour of new literature. I begin now with a psalm of the times:

["Chant de Guerre parisien"]

— Here is some prose on the future of poetry: — all ancient poetry led up to the Greek, harmonious Life. — From Greece down to the romantic movement — Middle Ages — there are writers and versifiers. From Ennius to Theroldus, from Theroldus to Casimir Delavigne, everything is rhymed prose, a game, the depravity and glory of innumerable idiot generations: Racine is the pure, the strong, the great. If anyone had breathed upon his rhymes, mixed up his hemistichs, the Divine Fool would have been as unknown today as the first author of *Origins** to come along. — After Racine the game goes stale. It has lasted two thousand years.

* Numerous historical studies had appeared under titles beginning, "The Origin of."

No joking, no paradox. My reason gives me more certitude on this subject than a Jeune-France poet would ever have had of anger. Besides, the *new* are free to execrate their ancestors: we are on our own ground, and we have the time.

No one has ever rightly judged romanticism. Who would have judged it? The Critics?? The Romantics, who prove so completely that song is so infrequently a work, that is, which is thought sung and understood by the singer?

For the "I" is someone else. That much is clear to me: I am a spectator at the blossoming of my own thought: I look at it and listen to it: I make a sweep with the bow and down in the depths the symphony begins to stir or comes in one leap upon the stage.

If the old fools had not found just the false signification of the Ego, we wouldn't have to be sweeping up these millions of skeletons which over an infinite time have been piling up the products of their one-eyed intelligence and declaring themselves the authors!

In Greece, as I have said, verse and lyre set the rhythms of Action. Afterward, music and rhyme are games, pastimes. The study of this past delights the curious: several are overjoyed to bring these antiquities back to life: — let them have it. Universal intelligence has always dropped its ideas naturally; men gathered up a share of these fruits of the mind: people acted according to, and wrote books about, them: that was the way the world went, man not working upon himself, not being yet awakened or not in the fullness of the great dream. Pen pushers, writers — but the author, the creator, the poet, this man has never existed.

The proper study of a man who wants to be a poet is himself, totally; he seeks his own soul, inspects it, tries it, learns it. As soon as he knows it he should cultivate it. That seems simple: in every mind there takes place a natural development; so many *egoists* proclaim that they are authors; there are many others who attribute their intellectual progress to themselves! — But it is a matter of making our soul monstrous: like the baby-snatchers,* indeed! Im-

* *Comprachicos*: criminals in Victor Hugo's *L'Homme qui rit,* who stole children and mutilated them so as to be able to exhibit them as freaks.

agine a man grafting and cultivating warts on the skin of his own face.

I say that we must be *voyant,* make ourselves *voyant.*

The poet makes himself *voyant* by *a long, immense, and calculated derailment of all the senses.* All the forms of love and suffering and madness; he seeks himself and exhausts in himself all the poisons, keeping only the quintessences. Unspeakable torture, in which he needs all the faith, all the superhuman strength, by which he becomes the great invalid, the great criminal, the great pariah, above all others — and the supreme Savant! — For he attains the *unknown*! Since he has cultivated his soul, which was rich to start with, more than anyone else! He reaches the unknown, and if, finally overwhelmed, he turns out to lose the meaning of his visions, at least he has seen them! Let him die in his surge through things unheard of and beyond naming: other horrible workers will come after him and begin at the horizons where he sank back!

— To be continued in six minutes —

I insert here a second psalm; it is not part of the argument: kindly lend a tolerant ear, — and all will be delighted. — I have the bow in hand and begin:

["Mes petites amoureuses"]

There you are. And please note that, if I didn't fear making you pay out more than sixty centimes in postage, — I, poor pauper who for seven months haven't had a red cent! — I would send you in addition my *Amants de Paris,* a hundred hexameters, Sir, and my *Mort de Paris,* two hundred hexameters!

— I go on:

So the poet is truly the fire-stealer.

He is responsible for humanity, even for the animals; he will have to invent something that can be touched, felt, heard; if what he brings back from *out there* has a form, he gives the form; if it is formless, he gives it non-form. To find a language; — Besides, every word being an idea, the time of a universal language will come. It takes an Academician, deader than a fossil, to bring a dictionary of any language whatsoever to a conclusion. There are weak characters who, if they just started to *think* about the first letter of the alphabet, would rapidly go stark mad!

This language will be of the soul, for the soul, summing up everything, perfumes, sounds, colors, thought seizing upon thought and drawing it on. The poet would define the quantity of unknown awakening in his time in the universal soul; he would give more — than the statement of his thought, and than his estimate of *his progress toward Progress.* The extra-normal becoming the norm, and being absorbed by all, he would really be *a multiplier of progress.*

This future will be materialist, as you see. — Always full of *Number* and *Harmony,* these poems will be made to last. — Fundamentally, this will still be something of Greek poetry.

Eternal art would have its civic role, since poets are citizens. Poetry will no longer just set action to rhythm; it will, itself, *take the lead.*

These poets will come to be! And when the infinite servitude of woman shall be broken, when she lives through and of herself, man, — up to now abominable, — having given her freedom, she will herself be a poet also. Woman will find the unknown! Will her universe of ideas be different from ours? — She will find curious things, plumbless, repulsive, delightful; we shall take them and take them in.*

Meanwhile, let us ask the *poet* for *something new,* — ideas and forms. The merely clever would think very soon they had met the requirement: — that's not what I mean.

The first romantics were *voyant* without really knowing it: The culture of their souls began by chance: like locomotives abandoned with steam up, which run a while by themselves. — Lamartine is sometimes a *voyant,* but strangled by his old form. Hugo, *too much the brain,*† really has vision in his latest volumes: *Les Misérables* is a true *poem.* I have the *Châtiments* before me; *Stella* just about shows how much Hugo could *see.* Too much Belmontet and Lamennais, too many Jehovahs and columns, monstrosities old and dead.

Musset is execrable fourteen times over for us, a generation which

* Rimbaud is punning mildly on *prendre* and *comprendre.*

† *Cabochard* is slang in French.

suffers and is caught up by visions, — and whom his angelic indolence has insulted! Oh! the flat tales and proverb-plays! Oh, the *Nuits*! Oh, *Rolla*, oh, *Namouna*, oh, the *Coupe*! All of it is French, that is, hateful in the ultimate degree; French, not Parisian! One more product of that odious genius which inspired Rabelais, Voltaire, Jean La Fontaine, as pointed out in M. Taine's commentary! * Springlike, the wit of Musset? Charming, his love? There you have it, painting done in enamel, solid poetry!

French poetry will be enjoyed for a long time, but only in France. Every grocer's clerk is up to unwinding a Rollaesque apostrophe, every seminarist confides his five hundred rimes to his secret notebook. At fifteen, these bursts of passion put the young in heat; at sixteen they are already satisfied to recite them *from the heart*; at eighteen, even seventeen, every schoolboy with the means plays Rolla, writes a Rolla! Perhaps some still die of it. Musset never managed to do anything: there were visions behind the gauze of the curtains: he shut his eyes. Frenchmen, strutters, the beautiful corpse, dragged from the pub to the schoolroom desk, is dead, and, from here on, let's not trouble ourselves to waken him with our abominations!

The second generation of romantics are very *voyant*: Théophile Gautier, Leconte de Lisle, Théodore de Banville. But inspecting the invisible, and hearing what was never heard being something else than restoring the spirit of things dead, Baudelaire is the first *voyant*, the king of poets, *a true God*. But he lived among too many artists; and his boasted form is shoddy. Inventing the unknown calls for new forms.

Broken in to the old forms, — among the innocents, A. Renaud, — he did his Rolla; — L. Grandet, — did his Rolla; — the Gauls and the Mussets, G. Lafenestre, Coran, Cl. Popelin, Soulary, L. Salles; the schoolboys, Marc. Aicard, Theuriet; the dead and the imbeciles, Autran, Barbier, L. Pichat, Lemoyne, the Deschamps, the Des Essarts; the journalists, L. Cladel, Robert Luzarches, X. de Ricard;

* Hippolyte Taine's *La Fontaine et ses fables* discusses the special, so-called "Gallic" mentality — compounded of common sense, gaiety, bawdiness, and a taste for satire — which these writers are supposed to represent.

the fantasists, C. Mendès; the bohemians; the women; the talents, Léon Dierx and Sully-Prudhomme, Coppée; the new school, called Parnassian, has two *voyants,* Albert Mérat and Paul Verlaine, a true poet. – There you are.

Thus I work at making myself *voyant.* And let us finish with a pious song.

["Accroupissements"]

You would be execrable not to reply: quick, for in a week I shall be in Paris, perhaps.

Farewell,

A. Rimbaud

Bibliographical Note

There are three excellent critical editions. Henri Bouillane de Lacoste pioneered with the *Poésies* (Paris: Mercure de France, 1939), followed in subsequent years by two further volumes. These were, in turn, the foundation for the edition by Rolland de Renéville and Jules Mouquet in the Pléiade series (1951, and, with revisions, 1954). Suzanne Bernard's *Oeuvres* (Paris: Garnier, 1960) profits by more recent research, and is especially rich in bibliography on disputed points; it contains, however, only a brief selection from the correspondence – for which the reader must return to the Pléiade edition.

The need for detailed bibliography is largely obviated by René Etiemble's comprehensive studies, *Le Mythe de Rimbaud* (Paris: Gallimard, I, *La Genèse du mythe*, 1954; II, *La Structure du mythe*, 1952; IV, *L'Année du centenaire*, 1961). The order of publication is correct as given here, the second volume having appeared before the first after presentation as a thesis at the Sorbonne. Etiemble's earlier *Rimbaud* (with Yassu Gauclère, Paris: Gallimard, 1936) gives his measure as a critic; his interpretation remains valuable although hampered by a rigid nineteenth-century positivism. His later writing combines deep devotion to scholarship with a polemic tone which many readers find distasteful: for an example, see his "Défense de déposer des ordures," a tract distributed in Charleville just before the centennial celebration and reprinted in *L'Année du centenaire* (page 122), in which he refers to certain current writings on Rimbaud as "turds" (*étrons*). The third volume of his series is not yet in print.

Bouillane de Lacoste's *Rimbaud et le problème des Illuminations* (Paris: Mercure de France, 1949) set off an extensive controversy which was remarkable both for the vehemence of the contributors and the inconclusiveness of the contributions. As an example of the neatness and tidiness with which it is no longer possible, thanks largely to his work, to pigeonhole the "stages" of Rimbaud's career, see Marguerite Mespoulet's article on him in *The Columbia Dictionary of Modern European Literature* (New York: Columbia University Press, 1947); it was prepared by a recognized and respected scholar. Suzanne Bernard, who had seen manuscripts available to Bouillane de Lacoste only in photocopy, followed his lead in the arrangement of her edition. Readers curious to see what difference the datings can make in the interpretation of individual pieces, particularly of the *Illuminations,* should read Antoine Adam, "L'Enigme des *Illuminations*" (*Revue des Sciences Humaines,* Nouvelle série, Fascicule 60, October–December 1950, 221–245); he proceeds upon the hypothesis that the datings proposed by Bouillane de Lacoste are correct and argues that if they are so, then various new interpretations become plausible. I take his caution to hide a firmer faith in these datings than appears openly in the article. Another hypothesis, that Rimbaud would be much likelier to write about what he had actually seen than what he had not, also underlies the study and is taken by its author for an axiom; he faces the eventual obligation to explain how Rimbaud ever wrote about a drunken boat without having voyaged on one.

Further studies of the possible datings will be found in Charles

Chadwick, *Etudes sur Rimbaud* (Paris: Nizet, 1960), who brings internal evidence against the views of Bouillane de Lacoste.

There are also serious doubts in the mind of Enid Starkie, whose biography, *Arthur Rimbaud* (London: Faber and Faber), still by far the best, should be read in the 1961 edition; Miss Starkie's opinions have varied, with the discovery of new materials, since her first edition (1938) and perhaps even more since her second (London: Hamish Hamilton, 1947); the reader has every reason to profit by her most mature conclusions.

So much of the effort of Rimbaud's biographers has been spent in correcting the statements of Paterne Berrichon that almost nothing either in his *Vie de Jean-Arthur Rimbaud* (Paris: Mercure de France, 1897), or in his *Jean-Arthur Rimbaud, le poète* (Paris: Mercure de France, 1912), stands unchallenged. Critics divide as to whether he did not know the truth or merely disliked telling it. A brief portrait-biography of him is given by Marguerite-Yerta Maléra in *Résonances autour de Rimbaud* (Paris: Editions du Myrte, 1946). It is easy to forget that this much-maligned man, who dropped everything to study Rimbaud's poetry, married the poet's sister, and devoted years of his life to furthering Rimbaud's reputation, was neither malicious nor stupid, although he may have been grievously henpecked; without him, despite his prejudices in favor of middle class respectability, Rimbaud might have taken far longer in attracting public attention. Madame Maléra's own views of Rimbaud are suspect to many because her passionate admiration blinds her at times to facts, but there is no reason for her to have distorted her picture of the poet's brother-in-law.

Classical examples of omnibus interpretations of the poetry are Rolland de Renéville, *Rimbaud le Voyant* (Paris: Au sans pareil, 1929; Paris: La Colombe, 1946), and Jacques Gengoux, *La Pensée poétique de Rimbaud* (Paris: Nizet, 1950). Each tries to show that Rimbaud's work presents a body of coherent thought and fails, according to a majority of critics, to prove his point. Rolland de Renéville's book has at most a heuristic value; Gengoux, quite apart from his alleged discovery of a systematic symbolism in Rimbaud, is interesting for his detection and discussion of sources.

More modest in their claims are the studies of Cecil A. Hackett, in particular *Rimbaud l'enfant* (Paris: Corti, 1949) and Wallace Fowlie's *Rimbaud, the Myth of Childhood* (London: D. Dobson, 1946). Hackett's psychoanalytical treatment is immensely rich in suggestion; Fowlie's reading of the *Illuminations* is especially helpful; both insist upon the element of infantilism in Rimbaud's work. Pierre Debray's *Rimbaud, le magicien disabusé* (Paris: Juillard, 1949) is an attempt to clarify Rimbaud by rearranging the texts on the assumption that the poet knew, at every point, exactly what he meant. The most complete attempt to make a *révolté* of Rimbaud is André Dhôtel, *Rimbaud et la révolte moderne* (Paris: Gallimard, 1952).

Perhaps the most interesting and sensitive discussion of Rimbaud to date is Yves Bonnefoy, *Rimbaud par lui-même* (Paris: Editions du Seuil, 1961). Bonnefoy disclaims knowing more about Rimbaud than anyone else, but brings to his reading of the poems the authority of an excellent poet. Despite the formula his book is condemned to follow because it belongs to a series, his suspicion of biographical explanations is exemplary. One is grateful, not knowing what Rimbaud meant by a given passage, to know at least what a poet of Bonnefoy's stature would have meant.

Among studies treating only a part of Rimbaud's work, Emilie Noulet, *Le Premier Visage de Rimbaud* (Brussels: Académie Royale de Langue et de Lettres Françaises, 1953), was long indispensable and is still extremely useful. Her discussion of the history of "Le Cœur supplicié" and its vicissitudes in the hands of interpreters is the most enlightening available – although one may disagree with her conclusion that Rimbaud must have made the trip to Paris at some other time than May 15, 1871.

Bruce A. Morrissette, *The Great Rimbaud Forgery* (St. Louis, Mo.: Washington University Press, 1956), summarizes all that is known about "La Chasse spirituelle" as well as much that is suspected.

Both Enid Starkie and Suzanne Bernard include selective bibliographies of periodical studies bearing upon matters of detail. To their lists should be added Bernard Weinberg, "Le Bateau ivre or the Limits of Symbolism" (*PMLA*, LXXII, March 1957, 165–193), for a scrupulously minute reading of the poem in question.

Readers interested in the general development of French lyric poetry will need Margaret Gilman, *The Idea of Poetry in France* (Cambridge, Mass.: Harvard University Press, 1958). June E. Downey's discussion of the psychology of literary creation is *The Creative Imagination: Studies in the Psychology of Literature* (New York: Harcourt Brace, 1929). She makes no specific mention of Rimbaud.

INDEX